THE TOP UK AIR FRYER COOKBOOK FOR BEGINNERS

Delicious, Easy, and Budget-Friendly Recipes Including Dinners, Lunches, Breakfasts, and More (With European Measurements and UK Ingredients)

By

Hannah Holmes

Table of Contents

ABOUT THE AUTHOR 6

INTRODUCTION 7

What Is an Air Fryer? 7
Benefits of Cooking With an Air Fryer 7
Things to Take Note of When Using an Air Fryer 7
Air Fryer FAQs 8

1 | BREAKFAST 11

1. Crunchy and Golden Scotch Eggs 12
2. Healthy Air Fryer Granola 12
3. Bacon-Wrapped Potato Fries 13
4. Strawberry and Cream Breakfast Scones 13
5. Ginger Blueberry Scones 14
6. Blueberry Cornbread 14
7. Breakfast Baked Potatoes 15
8. Air-Fried Bacon and Spinach Frittata 15
9. Egg, Bacon, and Cheese Breakfast Puff Cups 16
10. Air-Fried Cinnamon French Toast Sticks 16
11. Muffin Sandwich 17
12. Breakfast Pizza 17
13. Sweet and Spiced Breakfast Bacon 18
14. Stuffed French Toast With Toasted Pistachios 18
15. Sour Cream Coffee Cake 19
16. Air-Fried Sweet Potato and Bacon Hash 19
17. Air Fryer Sausage Breakfast Casserole 20
18. Air Fryer Bacon Egg Cups 20
19. Air Fryer Lemon and Blueberry Breakfast Bread 21
20. Air Fryer Cheesy Baked Eggs 21
21. Air Fryer Bacon and Brussels Sprouts 22
22. Air-Fried Scrambled Eggs With Chives 22
23. Air Fryer Eggs Casserole 23
24. Cheesy Sausage and Eggs 23
25. Cheese and Bacon Air-Fried Bake 24
26. Air Fryer Broccoli Quiche 24
27. Creamy Breakfast Eggs 25
28. Air-Fried Breakfast Potatoes 25
29. Air Fryer Breakfast Waffles 26
30. Bacon-Wrapped Avocado Fries 26
31. Air Fryer Hard-Boiled Eggs 27

2 | POULTRY 29

1. Hot and Creamy Chicken Thighs 30
2. Air Fryer Duck Breasts With Lemon-Butter Sauce 30
3. Lime Duck With Shallots and Butter Sauce 31
4. Turkey, Mushroom, and Pea Casserole 31
5. Air-Fried Chicken Thighs 32
6. Air Fryer Duck With Veggies 32
7. Air Fryer Pepperoni Chicken 33

8. Air Fryer Coconut Chicken 33
9. Lemon and Herb Air Fryer Chicken 34
10. Chicken, Peas, and Rice Casserole 34
11. Air Fryer Duck Breasts With Orange and Red Wine Sauce ...35
12. Duck Breast With Shallot-Butter Sauce 35
13. Air Fryer Lemon Chicken 36
14. Air Fryer Chicken With Green Onions and Coconut Sauce ...36
15. Cheese-Crusted Chicken 37
16. Air Fryer Chicken With Green Onion Sauce 37
17. Air Fryer Chicken Cacciatore 38
18. Air Fryer Turkey With Vegetables 38
19. Air Fryer Chicken With Garlic Sauce 39
20. Lemon Duck Breasts 39
21. Honey Duck Breasts 40
22. Air Fryer Chicken Thighs and Potatoes 40
23. Lemon Chicken With Capers 41
24. Air Fryer Chicken With Creamy Mushrooms 41
25. Simple Air-Fried Duck Breasts 42
26. Turkey With Lime and Green Onion Sauce 42
27. Air Fryer Turkey and Lentils Casserole 43
28. Simple Air Fryer Turkey Breasts 43
29. Lime Turkey Breasts 44
30. Delicious Air-Fried Duck Breasts 44

3 | FISH AND SEAFOOD 45

1. Air-Fried Cod With Peas 46
2. Air-Fried Trout in Lemon-Chive Butter Sauce 46
3. Coconut Salmon Casserole 47
4. Lime Salmon With Healthy Avocado Salad 47
5. Air Fryer Snapper Fillets With Veggies 48
6. Air-Fried Fish and Chips 48
7. Lemon and Cajun Air Fryer Salmon 49
8. Simple Air Fryer Catfish 49
9. Air-Fried Salmon Fish Cakes 50
10. Crispy Air Fryer Prawns With Hot and Sweet Sauce 50
11. Tasty Air-Fried Cod 51
12. Air-Fried Lemon Catfish 51
13. Cod Fillets With Pecans 52
14. Air Fryer Lemon Salmon 52
15. Spiced Cod in Lime and Plum Sauce 53
16. Simple Air-Fried Salmon With Fresh Scallions 53
17. Lemon and Chilli Tilapia 54
18. Cod in Lemony Tomato Sauce 54
19. Crab and Prawn Casserole 55
20. Air Fryer Seafood Casserole 55
21. Air-Fried Trout in Green Onion-Orange Sauce 56
22. Air Fryer Salmon in Blackberry Sauce 56
23. Delicious French Cod 57

24. Special Catfish Fillets 57

25. Air Fryer Tilapia in Coconut Sauce 58

26. Air Fryer Tilapia in Lemon-Chive Sauce 58

27. Air-Fried Orange-Honey Sea Bass With Lentils 59

28. Air Fryer Cod With Red Onions 59

4 | SNACKS AND APPETISERS 61

1. Cheesy Bacon-Stuffed Mushrooms 62

2. Air Fryer Courgette Chips 62

3. Air-Fried Sweet Potato Chips 63

4. Air-Fried Chickpeas 63

5. Air Fryer Cinnamon Biscuit Treats 64

6. Crispy Potato Wedges With Pesto 64

7. Bacon-Wrapped Dates 65

8. Soft and Buttery Garlic Rolls 65

9. Crispy Crab Wontons 66

10. Air Fryer Crunchy Onion Rings 66

11. Sweet and Sour Sticky Wings 67

12. Simple Butter Shortbread Cookies 67

13. Moist Chocolate Cake With Chocolate Chips 68

14. Nutty Apricot Bites 68

15. Berry Cheesecake Bars 69

16. Spongy Olive Cake 69

17. Strawberry and Cream Cheese Triangles 70

18. Crispy Tofu Bites 70

19. Classic Grilled Cheese Sandwich 71

20. Crunchy Fish Nuggets 71

21. Crispy Tortilla Chips 72

22. Air-Fried Cheese Bites 72

23. Pickle Fries 73

24. Fluffy Cinnamon Rolls 73

25. Yummy Air Fryer Apple Pies 74

26. Air Fryer Sweet Coconut Macaroons 74

27. Air Fryer Soufflé 75

28. Chocolate Muffins 75

29. Orange Berry Muffins 76

30. Choc 'N' Nut Banana Bread 76

5 | MEAT 77

1. Juicy Rib-Eye Steak 78

2. Tender Strip Steak With Chimichurri 78

3. Balsamic and Mustard Flank Steak 79

4. Classic Steak Sandwich 79

5. Juicy Italian Meatballs 80

6. Japanese-Style Meatballs 80

7. Sweetened Pork Chops 81

8. Delicious Boneless Pork Chops 81

9. Lamb With Orange and Olives 82

10. Mint-Infused Lamb Chops 82

11. Pork and Veggie Balls 83

12. Spicy Spanish Pork Burgers 83

13. Roasted Pepper Burgers 84

14. Crab-Stuffed Sirloin Steak 84

15. Coffee Rub Pork Tenderloins 85

16. Cuban-Style Pork Chops 85

17. Filet Mignon Wrapped in Bacon 86

18. Steak in Mushroom and Red Wine Sauce 86

19. Restaurant-Style Rib-Eye Steak 87

20. Spicy Rib-Eye Steak 87

21. Dark Spicy Hanger Steak 88

22. Creamy Black Pepper Steak 88

23. Pork Loin With Veggies 89

24. Air Fryer Beef and Broccoli 89

25. Beef Empanadas 90

26. Simple and Healthy Beef Burger 90

27. Herbed Beef Koftas 91

28. Lemon-Infused Lamb Chops 91

AIR FRYER COOKING CHART 92

ABOUT THE AUTHOR

A group of Chefs trying to make British cookbooks amazing again!

We know how busy you are, that is why we aim to make our recipes as easy, budget friendly and, of course, as delicious as possible, so you can cook up meals you look forward to that nourish you simultaneously. (And anyone you're cooking for!)

With every book we create we also include a Bonus fully coloured PDF meaning each recipe has a beautiful coloured photo!

We couldn't include them in the book due to printing costs and we wanted to keep the books as affordable as possible. We hope you enjoy!

Also, if you have any feedback on how we can improve this book & further books please email us that and we will make all the changes we can. Or, if you have any issues / troubles then simply email us those and our customer support team will be happy to help.

As already mentioned we can't add the colour photos inside the book due to printing costs (the book would be unaffordable), but any other improvements we would love to make with your help!

Our customer support email is **anthonypublishing123@gmail.com** – We hope to hear from you!
Happy Cooking!

INTRODUCTION

You've most likely heard of the phrase 'you are what you eat.' It comes as no surprise that if you eat healthy food, then you are going to have a healthy body; and in the same way, if you eat over-processed, fat-laden unhealthy foods, then it's going to show in your body.

Did you know that you can get started on a health journey, enjoy tasty comfort food, and get in the best shape of your life without breaking the bank? This is where we introduce the art of air frying!

This cooking guide is aimed at introducing to the air fryer – the appliance that everyone in the culinary and health and fitness world is talking about. We will start by first looking at what it is, how it works, the benefits of using it, tips for using and prepping your food before using it.

Next, we'll move to the second and fun section – the food section! Here we have 1,000 creative, delicious, and super-simple recipes that will make you fall in love with cooking. From scrumptious breakfasts to decadent desserts, from snacks to comfort lunches and dinners, you are going to enjoy the variety of vegan, vegetarian, and meat-lover options.

Without further ado, let's take a look at what an air fryer is and all you need to know about it. Then you'll be ready to put on your apron and get cooking!

What Is an Air Fryer?

This is a kitchen appliance that's used for cooking food using little to no oil. It is very similar to an oven as they are both used for roasting and baking, but an air fryer is considerably smaller compared to an oven.

Additionally, the heating elements of an air fryer are positioned at the top, and it also comes with a powerful fan that helps the air fryer heat up fast. It also distributes heat evenly, resulting in crisp, perfectly cooked food within a short timeframe and with very little oil.

The clean-up is also quite easy, considering most of the air fryer parts can be washed in the dishwasher. The air fryer comes with a manual that tells you which parts are dishwasher-safe.

An air fryer works by circulating very hot air (up to 205°C) around the food being cooked, which cooks food faster while creating the same, if not better, crispiness as would be attained using the traditional frying method.

Benefits of Cooking With an Air Fryer

Anyone who owns an air fryer will tell you that once you start cooking some of your favourite foods using an air fryer, there is no turning back! Here are some great reasons why you need to jump on the air fryer bandwagon ASAP!

Simple and versatile

Cooking using an air fryer is very easy and there are so many different features that you can use, depending on the model you get. Most air fryers have so many functions that you may actually never need to use your oven or microwave again. The process is actually really simple. All you need to do is put your food in the air fryer, set the timer and temperature, wait, and voilà! Food is ready and the clean-up is also easy.

Cook using very little oil

One of the biggest benefits of using an air fryer is that it uses very little oil compared to other cooking methods. Whether you are cooking French fries, fried chicken, or spring rolls, all you need is a tablespoon of oil – not cups of oil!

The hot air inside the air fryer circulates the heated oil droplets, keeping the inside of the food tender and the outside deliciously crisp. This significantly reduces your calorie intake, thus supporting your health journey.

Safer compared to a deep fryer

Using a deep fryer always comes with the risk of hot oil spills. An air fryer is the complete opposite as the cooking process takes place in a closed environment.

Can lower the risk of certain chronic ailments

For a long time, the consumption of fried food products has been shown to put a lot of pressure on vital organs such as the kidney, heart, and liver. This can lead to cardiovascular diseases, obesity, and certain cancers. Replacing fried foods with air-fried food can significantly reduce the chance of illnesses linked to fatty food.

Things to Take Note of When Using an Air Fryer

So, you have an air fryer but are not really sure about how to use it effectively. Here are a few tips that will come in handy.

Preheat before use

Just like an oven, it is important that you preheat your air fryer before adding in your food. This ensures that your food, whether frozen or at room temperature, starts to cook immediately.

Time and temperature

How do you know how hot your air fryer needs to be and how long to cook for? The recipes we have shared come with all that information. But in the event that you want to prepare a dish that you don't know what temperature to use and how long it will take to cook, the rule of thumb is to go with 180–205°C for 10 to 12 minutes.

Temperature should always stay the same, but the time will depend on the volume of the food you are cooking. A good tip is to look through your air fryer's viewing window regularly and check for brownness, as this is an indicator of the degree to which the food is done.

Ensure your food is dry before putting it in the air fryer

Pat your food dry before placing it in your air fryer's basket. This will ensure it's nice and crisp when ready, and you also don't have to worry about smoking and splattering. Use a kitchen towel to pat dry your food, especially a recipe that uses a marinade.

Add a tablespoon of oil or less when adding food to the air fryer

Brush or toss your food with a little oil. This will help it cook evenly with a crisp finish. Next, arrange the food in your basket without overcrowding it.

Placing food in the air fryer's basket

The one rule when cooking using an air fryer is never to put too much food in the basket. Remember, the air fryer relies on air circulation to cook your food. You therefore need to leave space for the air to travel. When you overcrowd your food, it won't cook evenly; the result will not be as crisp and you are likely to have some soggy patches.

Toss your food midway through the cooking time

This works perfectly for bite-sized foods such as French fries and chicken bites. This ensures even cooking and crispiness. For bigger portions of food, simply flip halfway through the cooking time.

Taking out your food

Well, isn't it just a case of pulling out the basket and taking out the food? For foods that don't contain a lot of fat, it's as simple as that. But when cooking foods that are fatty, such as pork, there will be a lot of drippings. Use some tongs to get the food out. Then, depending on whether you want to keep the dripping that collects at the bottom, you can reserve or toss them.

Clean after use

Clean your air fryer after every use, as most foods will leave behind some oil droplets or crumbs that, if not cleaned, will make your air fryer smoke the next time you turn it on. It's also easier to clean before food droppings get stuck. Remove the bottom tray together with the basket and clean according to the air fryer's user manual.

It's as simple as that!

Air Fryer FAQs

To help you better understand and enjoy your flashy cooking appliance, I will be helping you answer some of the commonly asked air fryer questions.

Can I use oil in my air fryer?

One of the main selling points of an air fryer is the fact that it allows cooking with little to no oil; so, yes, you can use oil in your air fryer. The amount will vary depending on what recipe you are preparing.

Some recipes, such as boiled eggs, pork chops, chicken, and steak, may not need any oil to be air fried; but this is fully dependent on the desired outcome of your recipe.

For you to get a delicious crispiness on some of your recipes, you will need a little spritz of oil. You can use your normal oil or cooking spray.

Is it safe to use parchment and foil paper in my air fryer?

Yes, it is. The only condition is you have food that is able to hold it down. Using parchment paper and foil will make cleaning up really easy. When using foil, do not put it in the air fryer when it is on 'preheat' mode as this could get the foil stuck in your air fryer element, which could easily start a fire or damage your appliance.

Can I cook frozen food in the air fryer?

Yes. You can cook frozen meats and veggies to perfection in your air fryer.

Can I make stews and soups in my air fryer?

It is not recommended to cook stews and soups in an air fryer because the air fryer fan blows hot air into the oven, and having liquids may cause a spillage that can result in an electric short when it comes into contact with the electrical components, which may also damage the oven.

How do I know my meats are cooked?

The Department for Environment, Food, and Rural Affairs (DEFRA) advises that all raw chops, veal, roast meats, lamb, beef, and pork should be cooked until they attain an internal temperature of 63°C, taken using a food thermometer before removing from the heat source.

Eggs and poultry should be cooked to 74°C, ground meats at 71°C, and seafood and shellfish at 63°C.

BREAKFAST

Don't Forget To Get The Color Images FREE!
Simply Scan The QR Code Below!

Hello! Please scan the QR code below to access your promised bonus of all our recipes with full colored photos & beautiful designs! It is the best we could do to keep the book as cheap as possible while providing the best value!

Also, once downloaded you can take the PDF with you digitally wherever you go- meaning you can cook these recipes wherever an Air Fryer is present!

STEP BY STEP Guide-

1. *Open Your Phones (Or Any Device You Want The Book On) Back Camera. The Back Camera Is The One You use as if you are taking a picture of someone.*

2. *Simply point your Camera at the QR code and 'tap' the QR code with your finger to focus the camera.*

3. *A link / pop up will appear. Simply tap that (and make sure you have internet connection) and the FREE PDF containing all of the colored images should appear.*

4. *If You Click On The File And It Says 'The File Is Too Big To Preview' Simply click 'Download' and it will download the full book onto your phone!*

5. *Now you have access to these FOREVER. Simply 'Bookmark' The tab it opened on, or download the document and take wherever you want.*

6. *Repeat this on any device you want it on!*

Any Issues / Feedback / Troubleshooting please email:
anthonypublishing123@gmail.com *and our customer service team will help you! We want to make sure you have the BEST experience with our books!*

1. Crunchy and Golden Scotch Eggs

These crunchy and golden scotch eggs are really simple to whip up and are perfect for breakfast, a snack, or even brunch. Hard-boiled eggs are covered with pork sausage and crushed cornflakes, then air fried to crisp and crunchy perfection!

PREPARATION TIME: 10 MINUTES
COOKING TIME: 18 MINUTES
PER SERVING (6): KCAL: 313; FAT: 22G; CARBS: 11G; PROTEIN: 17G; SUGARS: 2G; FIBRE: 0G.

INGRENKEDIENTS:

- 6 free-range eggs
- 450g pork sausage
- ¼ teaspoon sea salt
- ¼ teaspoon black pepper
- 50g crushed cornflakes
- 2 medium eggs
- Non-stick oil spray

INSTRUCTIONS:

Step 1: Place the 6 eggs into the air fryer basket and cook them at 135°C for 15 minutes.

Step 2: Gently remove the cooked eggs from the air fryer basket and place them in a medium bowl of icy water. This will make peeling pretty easy. Peel and set aside.

Step 3: Season the sausage meat with sea salt and black pepper, then divide it into 6 patties of even size. Flatten each portion of sausage, then place one cooked egg at the centre and very gently wrap the sausage around it. Lightly beat the 2 eggs in a shallow bowl and place the cornflake crumbs in another shallow bowl.

Step 4: Dip the sausage-wrapped eggs, one at a time, into the egg mixture, then dip into the cornflakes crumbs until fully coated. Do this for all the eggs, then carefully place them in the air fryer basket.

Step 5: Lightly spray the eggs with non-stick oil spray and cook at 205°C for 15 to 18 minutes, until the sausage is cooked through and the coating is crisp and golden.

Step 6: Serve hot and enjoy!

2. Healthy Air Fryer Granola

This sweet, fruity, and nutty homemade granola is such a breeze to make with only 15 minutes of cooking time! It's a great pantry staple that you can add to your breakfasts, brunches, and desserts, and great to snack on just as is. Enjoy!

PREPARATION TIME: 5 MINUTES
COOKING TIME: 18 MINUTES
PER SERVING (4): KCAL: 336; FAT: 19G; CARBS: 38G; PROTEIN: 7G; SUGARS: 17G; FIBRE: 5G.

INGREDIENTS:

- 180g rolled oats
- 50g dried blueberries
- 25g dried cranberries
- 50g dried cherries
- 1 teaspoon flax seed
- 20g sunflower seeds
- 40g hazelnuts, chopped
- 40g walnuts, chopped
- 40g almonds, chopped
- 35g coconut flakes
- 20g pumpkin seeds
- 2 teaspoons raw honey
- 6 teaspoons extra virgin olive oil
- 40g maple syrup
- ½ teaspoon vanilla extract
- ⅛ teaspoon ground cloves
- ½ teaspoon ground cinnamon

INSTRUCTIONS:

Step 1: In a medium bowl, mix all the dry ingredients.

Step 2: In a small bowl, whisk together the raw honey, vanilla extract, maple syrup, and oil until well combined.

Step 3: Add the honey mixture to the dry ingredients and stir until well combined.

Step 4: Preheat your air fryer to 175°C, and air fry the granola for 18 minutes, stirring halfway through the cooking time. The granola should be crunchy and golden brown.

Step 5: Allow the granola to cool completely before transferring to an airtight container for storage.

3. Bacon-Wrapped Potato Fries

Who can say no to anything bacon-wrapped? These savoury fries are crisp on the outside and beautifully soft on the inside. The ranch dressing is the cherry on top! Enjoy these fries for breakfast or as a snack.

PREPARATION TIME: 5 MINUTES
COOKING TIME: 15 MINUTES
PER SERVING (4): KCAL: 447; FAT: 19.4G; CARBS: 52.8G; PROTEIN: 16.5G; SUGARS: 4.7G; FIBRE: 7.8G.

INGRENKEDIENTS:

- 24 slices bacon
- 3 russet potatoes, washed
- Freshly ground black pepper, to taste
- Sea salt, to taste
- 1 tablespoon olive oil
- 80g ranch dressing, for serving

INSTRUCTIONS:

Step 1: Start by cutting your potatoes into quarters.

Step 2: Next, in a large bowl, combine the potato wedges, olive oil, sea salt, and black pepper. Toss well to ensure the potatoes are evenly coated.

Step 3: Wrap the bacon slices around each potato wedge until the whole potato is coated. You may have to use 2 slices of bacon per wedge.

Step 4: Arrange the wrapped potatoes in the air fryer basket, spacing them out, and cook at 205°C for 15 minutes.

Step 5: Serve hot with the ranch dressing.

4. Strawberry and Cream Breakfast Scones

Soft, flaky, and with a delicious burst of sweet strawberries with each bite. Enjoy these breakfast scones warm with your favourite jam or just as is with a hot cup of tea.

PREPARATION TIME: 10 MINUTES
COOKING TIME: 12 MINUTES
PER SERVING (4): KCAL: 410; FAT: 24.1G; CARBS: 41.6G; PROTEIN: 7G; SUGARS: 9.4G; FIBRE: 1.4G.

INGREDIENTS:

- 240g all-purpose flour
- ¼ teaspoon sea salt
- 2 teaspoons baking powder
- 50g granulated sugar
- 6 tablespoons butter, diced
- 2 teaspoons vanilla extract
- 2 large eggs
- 170ml heavy cream
- 70g fresh strawberries, chopped
- 1 tablespoon water
- Granulated sugar, for topping

INSTRUCTIONS:

Step 1: In a large bowl, sift together flour, sea salt, baking powder, and sugar, then whisk to combine.

Step 2: Fold in butter and mix with a hand blender until the mixture resembles coarse crumbs.

Step 3: Fold in the strawberries, then set aside.

Step 4: In a separate bowl, whisk together 1 egg, the heavy cream, and vanilla extract until well blended. Fold into the flour mixture to form a soft dough.

Step 5: Roll out the dough into a 2-inch thick circle, then cut out the scones using a cookie cutter.

Step 6: Whisk the remaining egg with 2 tablespoons of water in a small bowl.

Step 7: Brush each scone with the egg wash, then sprinkle with granulated sugar.

Step 8: Select the preheat function on your air fryer, set the temperature to 175°C, and press the Start/Pause button.

Step 9: Line the inner basket with baking paper and arrange the scones.

Step 10: Set the timer to 12 minutes and press the Start/Pause button.

Step 11: Check for doneness by inserting a cocktail stick at the centre of one scone. If it comes out clean, the scones are ready. If not, cook for 3 more minutes, then check again.

Step 12: Transfer the scones to a wire rack for them to cool completely.

5. Ginger Blueberry Scones

This recipe perfectly blends the tang of the lemon, silky sweetness of blueberries, and the subtle spicy kick of ginger in a simple and delicious treat that you can have for breakfast, dessert, brunch, or as a snack. Enjoy!

PREPARATION TIME: 10 MINUTES
COOKING TIME: 17 MINUTES
PER SERVING (6): KCAL: 434; FAT: 24.2G; CARBS: 47.2G; PROTEIN: 7.3G; SUGARS: 12.5G; FIBRE: 1.6G.

INGREDIENTS:

- 250g all-purpose flour
- ½ teaspoon sea salt
- 2 teaspoons baking powder
- 60g brown sugar
- 2 large eggs, divided
- 170ml heavy cream
- 6 tablespoons butter, sliced
- 2 teaspoons vanilla extract
- 4 teaspoons ginger, grated¬
- 1 teaspoon fresh lemon zest
- 75g fresh blueberries
- 1 tablespoon water
- Granulated sugar, for topping

INSTRUCTIONS:

Step 1: In a large bowl, sift together flour, sea salt, baking powder, and sugar until well combined.

Step 2: Fold in the butter, and mix with a hand blender until the mixture resembles coarse sand.

Step 3: Fold in the blueberries, lemon zest, and ginger, then set aside.

Step 4: In a separate bowl, beat together 1 egg, the heavy cream, and the vanilla extract until well combined. Fold into the flour mixture to form soft but pliable dough.

Step 5: Roll out the dough into 2-inch thickness, then cut out the scones using a cookie cutter.

Step 6: Whisk the remaining egg with a tablespoon of water in a small bowl.

Step 7: Brush each scone with the egg wash and sprinkle with granulated sugar.

Step 8: Select the preheat function on your air fryer, set the temperature to 175°C, and press the Start/Pause button.

Step 9: Line the inner basket with baking paper and insert the scones.

Step 10: Set the timer to 12 minutes and press the Start/Pause button.

Step 11: Check for doneness by inserting a cocktail stick at the centre of one scone. If it comes out clean, the scones are ready. If not, cook for 3 more minutes, then check again.

Step 12: When golden brown, transfer to a wire rack and serve warm.

6. Blueberry Cornbread

Light, more cake-like than bread-like, and with just the right amount of sweetness; you are going to love this blueberry cornbread. Serve it with your favourite fruit jam and enjoy!

PREPARATION TIME: 10 MINUTES
COOKING TIME: 45 MINUTES
PER SERVING (6): KCAL: 550; FAT: 25.6G; CARBS: 72.5G; PROTEIN: 8.6G; SUGARS: 31.4G; FIBRE: 2.9G.

INGREDIENTS:

- 190g all-purpose flour
- 120g cornmeal
- 170g brown sugar
- ¾ teaspoon sea salt
- 2 teaspoons baking powder
- 2 large free-range eggs
- 12 tablespoons unsalted butter, melted
- 250ml milk
- 150g blueberries

INSTRUCTIONS:

Step 1: Preheat your air fryer to 175°C.

Step 2: Spray a baking pan with olive oil cooking spray.

Step 3: In a large bowl, mix together the flour, cornmeal, brown sugar, sea salt, and baking powder until well combined.

Step 4: In a separate bowl, whisk together the melted butter, milk, and eggs until well blended. Pour into the flour mixture and mix to form a soft, slightly wet batter.

Step 5: Fold the blueberries into the batter until well combined, then transfer the batter to the baking pan.

Step 6: Set the timer to 45 minutes and press the Start/Pause button. A tester or cocktail stick inserted into the centre of the bread should come out clean, and the bread should be golden brown on the outside.

Step 7: Transfer to a wire rack, then slice and serve warm.

7. Breakfast Baked Potatoes

Simple to make and seasoned just right! These loaded breakfast potatoes are golden and crispy on the outside and very soft and fluffy on the inside. The creaminess of the sour cream, the meatiness of the salmon, and the freshness of the dill give you the best breakfast potato.

PREPARATION TIME: 5 MINUTES
COOKING TIME: 45 MINUTES
PER SERVING (1): KCAL: 262; FAT: 9.8G; CARBS: 34.8G; PROTEIN: 9.7G; SUGARS: 2.5G; FIBRE: 5.1G.

INGRENKEDIENTS:

- 6 medium russet potatoes, washed
- 6 slices smoked salmon
- 170ml sour cream
- 1 tablespoon olive oil
- ¼ teaspoon sea salt
- ¼ teaspoon black pepper
- Fresh dill, for garnish

INSTRUCTIONS:

Step 1: Preheat your air fryer to 205ºC.

Step 2: Drizzle the potatoes with olive oil and sprinkle with sea salt and pepper; transfer to the air fryer basket and cook for 45 minutes or until golden and crisp on the outside and soft on the inside.

Step 3: Remove the potatoes from the air fryer and let them cool for about 5 minutes. Make a slice along each potato, but be careful not to cut right through.

Step 4: Stuff each potato with smoked salmon, 2 tablespoons of sour cream, and fresh dill. Enjoy!

8. Air-Fried Bacon and Spinach Frittata

This filling protein- and veggie-rich frittata is a great breakfast or brunch option that will keep you energised and full all through the morning.

PREPARATION TIME: 3 MINUTES
COOKING TIME: 14 MINUTES
PER SERVING (4): KCAL: 411; FAT: 32.3G; CARBS: 3G; PROTEIN: 27.4G; SUGARS: 0.5G; FIBRE: 0.5G.

INGREDIENTS:

- 6 slices smoked bacon, diced
- 150g baby spinach
- 3 free-range eggs
- 3 tablespoons Parmesan cheese, grated
- 120ml heavy cream
- ¼ teaspoon sea salt
- ¼ teaspoon black pepper

INSTRUCTIONS:

Step 1: Select the preheat function on your air fryer, set the temperature to 175ºC, and press the Start/Pause button.

Step 2: Spray 3 ramekins with olive oil cooking spray and gently break an egg into each ramekin.

Step 3: Add the bacon to a skillet and cook over medium heat for about 5 minutes or until crispy.

Step 4: Add in the spinach and cook for about 2 minutes or until wilted.

Step 5: Stir in the Parmesan cheese and heavy cream and continue cooking for 3 minutes.

Step 6: Pour the bacon mixture onto each egg and place the ramekins into the air fryer.

Step 7: Set the timer to 4 minutes and press the Start/Pause button.

Step 8: Cook until the eggs are done to your desire, then season with sea salt and pepper.

9. Egg, Bacon, and Cheese Breakfast Puff Cups

Puff pastry with gooey cheese, eggs, and bacon! These are the tastiest and most convenient breakfast puff cups. Enjoy!

PREPARATION TIME: 5 MINUTES
COOKING TIME: 18 MINUTES
PER SERVING (4): KCAL: 485; FAT: 34.3G; CARBS: 28.6G; PROTEIN: 15.4G; SUGARS: 0.8G; FIBRE: 0.9G.

INGRENKEDIENTS:

* 1 sheet frozen puff pastry, thawed
* 4 tablespoons cheddar cheese, grated
* 4 tablespoons cooked bacon, chopped
* 4 eggs

INSTRUCTIONS:

Step 1: Preheat your air fryer to 205°C.

Step 2: Cut the pastry sheet into 4 squares and prick each a few times using a fork.

Step 3: Place the pastry squares into the air fryer basket. Cook for 8 minutes or until lightly browned.

Step 4: Open the basket and make an indentation in the centre of each pastry square; sprinkle bacon and cheese in each pastry square and crack an egg in each indentation.

Step 5: Return the basket to the air fryer and continue cooking for 10 minutes or until the egg is done to your desire.

10. Air-Fried Cinnamon French Toast Sticks

Dessert for breakfast? These air-fried cinnamon French toast sticks are easy to whip up and taste so good, with the cinnamon and honey blending perfectly. They are perfect for breakfast, brunch, or dessert. Enjoy!

PREPARATION TIME: 5 MINUTES
COOKING TIME: 10 MINUTES
PER SERVING (2): KCAL: 239; FAT: 6.2G; CARBS: 38G; PROTEIN: 8.8G; SUGARS: 28.3G; FIBRE: 1G.

INGREDIENTS:

* 4 slices white bread
* 2 free-range eggs
* 60ml milk
* 1 tablespoon raw honey
* ½ teaspoon vanilla extract
* Olive oil cooking spray
* 3 tablespoons brown sugar
* 1 teaspoon ground cinnamon
* Powdered sugar, for dusting
* Raw honey, for serving

INSTRUCTIONS:

Step 1: Cut each bread slice into 3 pieces and set aside.

Step 2: In a bowl, beat together the eggs, raw honey, vanilla extract, and milk until well combined.

Step 3: Select the preheat function on your air fryer, set the temperature to 175°C, and press the Start/Pause button.

Step 4: Dip the breadsticks into the milk-egg mix and place them in the air fryer basket lined with parchment paper. Spray with olive oil cooking spray.

Step 5: Set the timer to 10 minutes and press the Start/Pause button. Flip halfway through and cook until crispy and golden brown on the outside.

Step 6: Mix together the cinnamon and sugar in a small bowl and sprinkle over the breadsticks.

Step 7: Serve the breadsticks drizzled with raw honey.

11. Muffin Sandwich

This English muffin sandwich is really simple to make and insanely tasty. Ready in 15 minutes, this muffin sandwich is filling and the perfect way to start your day.

PREPARATION TIME: 5 MINUTES
COOKING TIME: 10 MINUTES
PER SERVING (4): KCAL: 418; FAT: 6.2G; CARBS: 23.2G; PROTEIN: 25.4G; SUGARS: 2.6G; FIBRE: 2.1G.

INGRENKEDIENTS:

*   1 English muffin, halved
*   1 slice bacon
*   1 slice white cheddar cheese
*   1 large egg
*   1 tablespoon hot water
*   ¼ teaspoon sea salt
*   ¼ teaspoon black pepper
*   Olive oil cooking spray

INSTRUCTIONS:

Step 1: Spray each ramekin with olive oil cooking spray and place in the air fryer.

Step 2: Select the preheat function on your air fryer, set the temperature to 175°C, and press the Start/Pause button.

Step 3: Place the bacon and cheese onto one half of the English muffin.

Step 4: Place both English muffin halves into the air fryer.

Step 5: Add the egg and hot water into the preheated ramekin and sprinkle with sea salt and pepper.

Step 6: Select the 'Toast' function on your air fryer, set the timer to 10 minutes, then press the Start/Pause button.

Step 7: Remove the muffins after 7 minutes of cooking and let the egg cook for the full duration.

Step 8: To assemble the sandwich, place the egg over the muffin and serve immediately.

12. Breakfast Pizza

Power your morning with a healthy, high protein pizza that is easy to make and very delicious.

PREPARATION TIME: 5 MINUTES
COOKING TIME: 8 MINUTES
PER SERVING (2): KCAL: 296; FAT: 11G; CARBS: 35.5G; PROTEIN: 14.2G; SUGARS: 2.2G; FIBRE: 1.4G.

INGREDIENTS:

*   2 teaspoons extra virgin olive oil
*   1 7-inch pre-cooked pizza crust
*   30g low-moisture mozzarella cheese, grated
*   2 slices smoked ham, diced
*   1 egg
*   1½ tablespoons coriander, chopped

INSTRUCTIONS:

Step 1: Select the preheat function on your air fryer, set the temperature to 175°C, then press the Start/Pause button.

Step 2: Brush the pizza crust with extra virgin olive oil.

Step 3: Place the smoked ham and mozzarella cheese onto the crust.

Step 4: Place the pizza into the air fryer and set the timer to 8 minutes; press the Start/Pause button.

Step 5: Remove the pizza after 5 minutes and crack the egg on top.

Step 6: Return the pizza and finish cooking.

Step 7: Serve the breakfast pizza garnished with chopped coriander.

13. Sweet and Spiced Breakfast Bacon

This candied bacon is a sweet and spicy spin on traditional bacon. You can have it for breakfast, on your favourite burger, or in a sandwich.

PREPARATION TIME: 2 MINUTES
COOKING TIME: 8 MINUTES
PER SERVING (2): KCAL: 233; FAT: 16.4G; CARBS: 6.6G; PROTEIN: 14.5G; SUGARS: 4.6G; FIBRE: 1G.

INGRENKEDIENTS:

- 1 tablespoon dark brown sugar
- 2 teaspoons chilli powder
- ¼ teaspoon ground cumin
- ¼ teaspoon cayenne pepper
- 4 slices bacon, halved

INSTRUCTIONS:

Step 1: Select the preheat function on your air fryer, set the temperature to 175°C, and press the Start/Pause button.

Step 2: In a small bowl, mix together the cayenne pepper, cumin, chilli powder, and dark brown sugar until well combined.

Step 3: Dredge bacon slices in the spice mixture until well coated.

Step 4: Place the coated bacon into the air fryer and select the 'Bacon' function. Press the Start/Pause button.

Step 5: When done, remove and serve warm.

14. Stuffed French Toast With Toasted Pistachios

Elegant, delicious, and super simple to make, this stuffed French toast with toasted pistachios is perfect for breakfast, brunch, or dessert. The saltiness of the nuts goes really well with the sweetness and creaminess of the French toast.

PREPARATION TIME: 4 MINUTES
COOKING TIME: 10 MINUTES
PER SERVING (1): KCAL: 687; FAT: 40.3G; CARBS: 69.1G; PROTEIN: 19.7G; SUGARS: 57.4G; FIBRE: 3.5G.

INGREDIENTS:

- 1 slice brioche bread
- 30g cream cheese
- 2 tablespoons heavy cream
- 2 tablespoons milk
- 2 eggs
- ½ teaspoon vanilla extract
- 1 teaspoon cinnamon
- 3 tablespoons sugar
- Olive oil cooking spray
- 20g toasted pistachios, chopped
- 1 tablespoon raw honey

INSTRUCTIONS:

Step 1: Select the preheat function on your air fryer, set the temperature to 175°C, and press the Start/Pause button.

Step 2: Using a knife, make a slit in the middle of brioche slice, and stuff it with the cream cheese.

Step 3: In a large bowl, whisk together the heavy cream, milk, eggs, vanilla extract, cinnamon, and sugar until well combined.

Step 4: Place the stuffed toast into the egg mixture and let it soak for about 10 seconds.

Step 5: Spray both sides of the toast with olive oil cooking spray and place it inside the preheated air fryer. Set the timer to 10 minutes and press the Start/Pause button.

Step 6: When done cooking, carefully remove the toast from the air fryer and place on a platter.

Step 7: Serve the toast topped with chopped toasted pistachios and drizzled with raw honey. Enjoy!

15. Sour Cream Coffee Cake

This flaky crumb cake with a deliciously crunchy pecan topping is incredibly simple to make and makes breakfast all the more special. With this recipe, one slice may not be enough!

PREPARATION TIME: 15 MINUTES
COOKING TIME: 35 MINUTES
PER SERVING (6): KCAL: 477; FAT: 31G; CARBS: 47G; PROTEIN: 6G; SUGARS: 28G; FIBRE: 3G.

INGRENKEDIENTS:

Cake:

* 120ml sour cream
* 1 free-range egg
* 110g brown sugar
* ½ teaspoon vanilla extract
* 110g softened butter
* 125g all-purpose flour
* ¼ teaspoon baking soda
* ½ teaspoon baking powder
* ½ teaspoon kosher salt

Topping:

* 100g pecans, chopped
* 60g brown sugar
* 1 teaspoon cinnamon

INSTRUCTIONS:

Step 1: Preheat your air fryer to 160°C and grease an 8-inch baking pan.

Step 2: In a small bowl, mix together the topping ingredients until well combined.

Step 3: In a large bowl, beat together brown sugar and butter until light and fluffy; mix in the egg, sour cream, and vanilla extract until well combined.

Step 4: In another bowl, mix the flour, salt, baking powder, and baking soda; add the sour cream mix and stir to combine well.

Step 5: Transfer half of the batter into the baking pan and smoothen the top, sprinkle with half of the topping mixture, and layer on the remaining batter followed by the remaining topping.

Step 6: Place into the air fryer and set the timer to 35 minutes or until a tester (for example, a cocktail stick) inserted in the centre comes out clean.

Step 7: Remove from the air fryer and let it cool completely before serving.

16. Air-Fried Sweet Potato and Bacon Hash

This air-fried sweet potato and bacon hash is satisfying and delicious with crispy sweet potatoes and bacon, caramelised onions, and seasoned perfectly. And what's more, it can be ready in as little as 35 minutes.

PREPARATION TIME: 15 MINUTES
COOKING TIME: 20 MINUTES
PER SERVING (4): KCAL: 199; FAT: 11G; CARBS: 20G; PROTEIN: 5G; SUGARS: 10G; FIBRE: 2G.

INGREDIENTS:

* 3 medium sweet potatoes
* 2 tablespoons brown sugar
* 4 slices bacon, diced
* 1 large red onion, diced
* 1 teaspoon dried rosemary
* 2 tablespoons extra virgin olive oil
* ¼ teaspoon sea salt
* ¼ teaspoon black pepper

INSTRUCTIONS:

Step 1: Preheat your air fryer to 205°C.

Step 2: Mix together the brown sugar and bacon until well coated.

Step 3: In a separate bowl, mix the red onion, sweet potatoes, olive oil, sea salt, rosemary, and pepper until the potatoes are well coated.

Step 4: Transfer the sweet potato mix to the air fryer basket and cook for 8 minutes.

Step 5: Take out the air fryer basket and add in the bacon mixture. Continue cooking for another 6 minutes.

Step 6: Stir the mixture and cook for another 7 minutes or until the potatoes are cooked through and the bacon is crispy and golden brown.

17. Air Fryer Sausage Breakfast Casserole

If you are looking for a special breakfast and brunch, this is it. You can make it in the morning or the night before and enjoy with a cup of tea or coffee.

PREPARATION TIME: 10 MINUTES
COOKING TIME: 20 MINUTES
PER SERVING (6): KCAL: 517; FAT: 37G; CARBS: 27G; PROTEIN: 21G; SUGARS: 4G; FIBRE: 3G.

INGRENKEDIENTS:

- 4 free-range eggs
- 500g hash browns
- 1 large red onion, chopped
- 500g breakfast sausage, ground
- 1 yellow bell pepper, diced
- 1 red bell pepper, diced
- 1 green bell pepper, diced

INSTRUCTIONS:

Step 1: Line the basket of your fryer with aluminium foil and add in the hash browns and top with sausage, peppers, and sliced red onions.

Step 2: Preheat your air fryer to 175°C.

Step 3: Set the timer to 10 minutes and press the Start/Pause button. Stir the casserole to mix well and continue cooking for another 10 minutes.

Step 4: Remove from the air fryer and season with sea salt and pepper.

18. Air Fryer Bacon Egg Cups

These air fryer bacon eggs cups are the perfect base for leftover veggies. Ready in only 15 minutes, these simple bacon egg cups make the best breakfast.

PREPARATION TIME: 5 MINUTES
COOKING TIME: 10 MINUTES
PER SERVING(4): KCAL: 126; FAT: 9G; CARBS: 1G; PROTEIN: 10G; SUGARS: 0G; FIBRE: 0G.

INGREDIENTS:

- 4 slices bacon
- 4 free-range eggs
- ¼ teaspoon sea salt
- ¼ teaspoon black pepper

INSTRUCTIONS:

Step 1: Make a basket of bacon by lining the walls of a muffin tray with bacon slices.

Step 2: Place the muffins in the air fryer basket and cook at 205°C for 5 minutes.

Step 3: Remove the muffin tray from the air fryer and crack an egg into the centre of each tin. Season with sea salt and pepper.

Step 4: Return to the air fryer and cook for another 5 minutes.

Step 5: Remove and serve warm.

19. Air Fryer Lemon and Blueberry Breakfast Bread

Swap regular plain bread for this delicious lemon and blueberry bread that is soft with a delicious berry or two in every bite.

PREPARATION TIME: 20 MINUTES
COOKING TIME: 20 MINUTES
PER SERVING (8): KCAL: 289; FAT: 13.1G; CARBS: 39.7G; PROTEIN: 4.6G; SUGARS 20.8G; FIBRE: 0.9G.

INGRENKEDIENTS:

- 110g butter
- 150g of sugar
- 2 eggs
- 120ml milk
- 190g all-purpose flour
- 1 teaspoon baking powder
- 1 teaspoon salt
- 2 tablespoons lemon juice
- 90g fresh blueberries

INSTRUCTIONS:

Step 1: In a bowl, cream together butter and brown sugar, then whisk in the flour, fresh lemon juice, sea salt, and baking powder until well blended.

Step 2: Fold in the blueberries and transfer the batter to a greased baking pan.

Step 3: Place the pan into the air fryer and cook at 160°C for 20 minutes or until a tester (for example, a cocktail stick) placed in the centre comes out clean. Remove from the air fryer and place on a wire rack to cool.

Step 4: Serve warm with your favourite fruit jam.

20. Air Fryer Cheesy Baked Eggs

Eggs for breakfast are the natural way to start the day. Add some cheese on top and you have a winner. Serve with a slice of your favourite toast and a cup of tea.

PREPARATION TIME: 5 MINUTES
COOKING TIME: 16 MINUTES
PER SERVING (2): KCAL: 194; FAT: 13.8G; CARBS: 1.3G; PROTEIN: 16.1G; SUGARS 1.1G; FIBRE: 0.1G.

INGREDIENTS:

- Olive oil cooking spray
- 4 large free-range eggs
- 30g gouda cheese, grated
- ¼ teaspoon sea salt
- ¼ teaspoon black pepper

INSTRUCTIONS:

Step 1: Grease 2 ramekins with olive oil cooking spray and 2 eggs in each, and top each with 1 tablespoon of gouda cheese. Season with sea salt and pepper.

Step 2: Place the ramekins inside the air fryer basket and cook at 205°C for 16 minutes or until the eggs are done to your desire.

Step 3: Serve hot.

21. Air Fryer Bacon and Brussels Sprouts

Spruce up your veggie mornings with this bacon and Brussels sprouts recipe. Crisp and crunchy on the outside and soft and tender on the inside with a cheesy garnish, you are going to love every bite of this dish.

PREPARATION TIME: 15 MINUTES
COOKING TIME: 35 MINUTES
PER SERVING (8): KCAL: 285; FAT: 23G; CARBS: 11G; PROTEIN: 11G; SUGARS: 2G; FIBRE: 4G.

INGRENKEDIENTS:

* 1kg Brussels sprouts, trimmed
* 500g bacon
* 50g grated Parmesan cheese, for serving

INSTRUCTIONS:

Step 1: Arrange the bacon slices in the air fryer basket without overlapping.

Step 2: Cook at 180°C for about 15 minutes, turning once halfway through.

Step 3: Place the trimmed Brussels sprouts into a large bowl.

Step 4: Remove the bacon from the air fryer and cut into large pieces, discard the excess grease, and add to the bowl with the Brussels sprouts. Toss to combine well and cook at 205°C for 20 minutes or until the bacon is crispy and golden brown and the Brussels sprouts are cooked through. Serve hot and sprinkle with grated Parmesan.

22. Air-Fried Scrambled Eggs With Chives

Buttery, creamy, and fluffy, these air-fried scrambled eggs with chives are delicious, easy to prepare, and packed with protein. The best way to start your day!

PREPARATION TIME: 1 MINUTES
COOKING TIME: 6 MINUTES
PER SERVING (2): KCAL: 264; FAT: 21.4G; CARBS: 6.4G; PROTEIN: 13.6G; SUGARS: 4.5G; FIBRE: 1.6G.

INGREDIENTS:

* 30g butter
* 3 large free-range eggs
* 120ml milk
* ½ teaspoon sea salt
* ¼ teaspoon black pepper
* 120g chives, chopped

INSTRUCTIONS:

Step 1: Add the butter to an aluminium tray and place it into the bottom of your fryer.

Step 2: In a bowl, whisk together the chopped chives, milk, eggs, sea salt, and pepper until well combined.

Step 3: Pour the egg mixture into the tray inside your air fryer.

Step 4: Cook in the air fryer at 180°C (stopping to stir the eggs every 2 minutes) for about 6 minutes or until you achieve your desired doneness.

23. Air Fryer Eggs Casserole

This air fryer eggs casserole combines delicious flavours and textures to make the perfect breakfast meal. The best thing about it is you can make it the night before and reheat it for an easy weekday breakfast!

PREPARATION TIME: 10 MINUTES
COOKING TIME: 25 MINUTES
PER SERVING (6): KCAL: 300; FAT: 5G; CARBS: 13G; PROTEIN: 6G; SUGARS: 1G; FIBRE: 8G.

INGRENKEDIENTS:

- 1 tablespoon extra virgin olive oil
- 12 eggs
- 500g ground turkey
- 1 sweet potato, diced
- ½ teaspoon chilli powder
- 250g baby spinach
- 2 tomatoes, chopped
- ¼ teaspoon sea salt
- ¼ teaspoon black pepper

INSTRUCTIONS:

Step 1: In a large bowl, whisk together the eggs, baby spinach, turkey, sweet potato, sea salt, chilli powder, and pepper.

Step 2: Pour the mix into a baking dish that fits into your air fryer.

Step 3: Cook at 200°C for 25 minutes.

Step 4: Divide among the serving plates and serve.

24. Cheesy Sausage and Eggs

This is a tasty frittata of eggs, diced sausage, cheese, and milk. Great for a weekend breakfast! Feel free to use as much of your favourite cheese as you like for this recipe.

PREPARATION TIME: 10 MINUTES
COOKING TIME: 25 MINUTES
PER SERVING (4): KCAL: 745; FAT: 59G; CARBS: 5G; PROTEIN: 48G; SUGARS: 4G; FIBRE: 0G.

INGREDIENTS:

- 1 tablespoon extra virgin olive oil
- 300g sausage, diced
- 250ml milk
- 8 free-range eggs
- 250g mozzarella cheese, grated
- 250g cheddar cheese, grated
- ¼ teaspoon sea salt
- ¼ teaspoon black pepper

INSTRUCTIONS:

Step 1: Heat olive oil in a skillet and cook the sausage over medium heat for about 5 minutes.

Step 2: In a large bowl, whisk together the eggs, sausages, mozzarella, cheddar, milk, sea salt, and pepper until well combined.

Step 3: Add the mixture to a baking dish that fits into your air fryer.

Step 4: Cook at 190°C for 20 minutes.

Step 5: Divide the meal among serving plates and serve. Enjoy!

25. Cheese and Bacon Air-Fried Bake

Perfectly seasoned, this breakfast bake is simple, tasty, meaty, and very filling. You can prepare it ahead of time if you have a busy morning ahead. Perfect for breakfast, brunch, or even lunch, you can eat this bake as is or serve it alongside toast, scones, or muffins.

PREPARATION TIME: 10 MINUTES
COOKING TIME: 30 MINUTES
PER SERVING (6): KCAL: 578; FAT: 46G; CARBS: 5G; PROTEIN: 36G; SUGARS: 4G; FIBRE: 1G.

INGRENKEDIENTS:

- 4 bacon slices
- 500g breakfast sausage, diced
- 600g cheddar cheese, grated
- 500ml milk
- 2 eggs
- ½ teaspoon onion powder
- 3 tablespoons parsley, chopped
- ¼ teaspoon sea salt
- ¼ teaspoon black pepper

INSTRUCTIONS:

Step 1: Add the bacon to a skillet and cook for about 10 minutes or until crispy and golden brown. Crumble and set aside.

Step 2: In a large bowl, whisk the eggs, cheese, milk, onion powder, parsley, sea salt, and pepper until well combined.

Step 3: Spread the bacon and sausages in a baking dish that fits into your air fryer.

Step 4: Pour the egg mixture over the bacon and cook at 160°C for 20 minutes.

Step 5: Divide the casserole among serving plates and serve right away.

26. Air Fryer Broccoli Quiche

Looking for a healthy and easy way of making your eggs? This air fryer broccoli quiche is a tasty and easy recipe. Cooking eggs in the air fryer makes them fluffy and light and the veggies make this breakfast all the more healthier and delicious.

PREPARATION TIME: 10 MINUTES
COOKING TIME: 20 MINUTES
PER SERVING (2): KCAL: 167; FAT: 8G; CARBS: 16G; PROTEIN: 11G; SUGARS: 8G; FIBRE: 4G.

INGREDIENTS:

- 3 carrots, chopped
- 1 tomato, chopped
- 1 broccoli head, chopped into florets
- 50g cheddar cheese, grated
- 2 eggs
- 60ml milk
- 1 teaspoon parsley, chopped
- 1 teaspoon thyme, chopped
- ¼ teaspoon sea salt
- ¼ teaspoon black pepper

INSTRUCTIONS:

Step 1: In a large bowl, whisk together the eggs, milk, thyme, parsley, sea salt, and pepper until well combined.

Step 2: Add the broccoli florets, tomatoes, and carrots in a steamer, and steam for 2 minutes.

Step 3: Transfer the steamed veggies to a baking dish that fits into your air fryer.

Step 4: Pour the egg mix over the veggies and sprinkle with grated cheddar cheese.

Step 5: Cook at 180°C for 20 minutes.

Step 6: Divide the quiche among serving plates and serve.

27. Creamy Breakfast Eggs

There's something about starting your first meal of the day on the right foot. These creamy breakfast eggs will do just that. Serve with toast and a cup of tea, and enjoy the rest of your day!

PREPARATION TIME: 10 MINUTES
COOKING TIME: 12 MINUTES
PER SERVING (4): KCAL: 263; FAT: 5G; CARBS: 12G; PROTEIN: 15G; SUGARS: 3G; FIBRE: 8G.

INGRENKEDIENTS:

- 30g butter, melted
- 2 ham slices
- 50g Parmesan cheese, grated
- 30ml heavy cream
- 4 eggs
- ¼ teaspoon sea salt
- ¼ teaspoon black pepper
- 2 tablespoons chives, chopped
- ¼ teaspoon smoked paprika

INSTRUCTIONS:

Step 1: Lightly grease the air fryer basket with melted butter.

Step 2: Arrange the ham in the prepared air fryer basket in a single layer.

Step 3: In a bowl, whisk together the heavy cream, eggs, sea salt, and pepper until well combined. Pour over the ham.

Step 4: Sprinkle with Parmesan cheese and cook at 160°C for 12 minutes.

Step 5: Remove the cheesy eggs from the air fryer and divide among serving plates. Sprinkle each serving with chopped chives and paprika. Enjoy!

28. Air-Fried Breakfast Potatoes

Delicious, easy, and quick to make, these wonderfully seasoned breakfast potatoes are crisp on the outside, fluffy on the inside, and are ready in only 15 minutes!

PREPARATION TIME: 2 MINUTES
COOKING TIME: 15 MINUTES
PER SERVING (2): KCAL: 375; FAT: 7G; CARBS: 67G; PROTEIN: 13G; SUGARS: 25G; FIBRE: 13G.

INGREDIENTS:

- 5 medium potatoes, peeled and diced
- 1 tablespoon extra virgin olive oil
- ½ teaspoon garlic powder
- ½ teaspoon smoked paprika
- ½ teaspoon kosher salt
- ¼ teaspoon black pepper

INSTRUCTIONS:

Step 1: Preheat your air fryer to 200°C.

Step 2: In a large bowl, toss together the potatoes, extra virgin olive oil, garlic powder, paprika, sea salt, and pepper until well coated.

Step 3: Spray the air fryer basket with olive oil cooking spray and add in the potatoes.

Step 4: Set the timer to 15 minutes and press the Start/ Pause button.

Step 5: When done, transfer to a plate and serve.

29. Air Fryer Breakfast Waffles

Looking for the quickest breakfast for those days when you are extremely busy? These breakfast waffles are exactly what you need. Simply pop your frozen waffles into your air fryer and have them ready in 6 minutes.

PREPARATION TIME: 2 MINUTES
COOKING TIME: 6 MINUTES
PER SERVING (1): KCAL: 180; FAT: 6G; CARBS: 27G; PROTEIN: 4G; SUGARS: 15G; FIBRE: 6G.

INGRENKEDIENTS:

- 2 frozen waffles
- Olive oil cooking spray

INSTRUCTIONS:

Step 1: Place the waffles in your air fryer basket and make sure they do not overlap.

Step 2: Set the air fryer timer to 4 minutes and press the Start/Pause button. Air fry at 180°C. Flip them over and cook for another 2 minutes or until golden brown.

30. Bacon-Wrapped Avocado Fries

Who can say no to anything bacon-wrapped? This savoury fries are crisp on the outside and beautifully soft on the inside. The ranch dressing is the cherry on top! Enjoy these fries for breakfast or as a snack.

PREPARATION TIME: 5 MINUTES
COOKING TIME: 5 MINUTES
PER SERVING 24 FRIES (12 SERVINGS): KCAL: 120; FAT: 11G; CARBS: 3G; PROTEIN: 4G; SUGARS: 0G; FIBRE: 2G.

INGREDIENTS:

- 24 slices bacon
- 3 avocados
- 60ml ranch dressing

INSTRUCTIONS:

Step 1: Preheat your air fryer to 200°C.

Step 2: Cut each avocado into 8 wedges and wrap each with one slice of bacon. Place them on a baking sheet, seam-side down.

Step 3: Set the timer to 15 minutes and press the Start/Pause button.

Step 4: Remove from the air fryer and serve with the ranch dressing.

31. Air Fryer Hard-Boiled Eggs

Looking for an easy way of boiling your eggs? These air fryer hard-boiled eggs are effortless. Once you boil your eggs in your air fryer, you will never look back!

PREPARATION TIME: 2 MINUTES
COOKING TIME: 15 MINUTES
PER SERVING (4): KCAL: 72; FAT: 5G; CARBS: 1G; PROTEIN: 6G; SUGARS: 0.2G; FIBRE: 0G.

INGRENKEDIENTS:

* 4 large eggs
* Water and ice

INSTRUCTIONS:

Step 1: Preheat your air fryer to 130°C.

Step 2: Place the eggs in the air fryer basket and set the timer to 15 minutes.

Step 3: When done, transfer the eggs to an ice bath to halt the cooking.

Step 4: Peel the eggshell and serve right away!

POULTRY

Don't Forget To Get The Color Images FREE!
Simply Scan The QR Code Below!

Hello! Please scan the QR code below to access your promised bonus of all our recipes with full colored photos & beautiful designs! It is the best we could do to keep the book as cheap as possible while providing the best value!

Also, once downloaded you can take the PDF with you digitally wherever you go- meaning you can cook these recipes wherever an Air Fryer is present!

STEP BY STEP Guide-

1. *Open Your Phones (Or Any Device You Want The Book On) Back Camera. The Back Camera Is The One You use as if you are taking a picture of someone.*

2. *Simply point your Camera at the QR code and 'tap' the QR code with your finger to focus the camera.*

3. *A link / pop up will appear. Simply tap that (and make sure you have internet connection) and the FREE PDF containing all of the colored images should appear.*

4. *If You Click On The File And It Says 'The File Is Too Big To Preview' Simply click 'Download' and it will download the full book onto your phone!*

5. *Now you have access to these FOREVER. Simply 'Bookmark' The tab it opened on, or download the document and take wherever you want.*

6. *Repeat this on any device you want it on!*

Any Issues / Feedback / Troubleshooting please email:
anthonypublishing123@gmail.com *and our customer service team will help you! We want to make sure you have the BEST experience with our books!*

1. Hot and Creamy Chicken Thighs

Delicious and easy-to-prepare crispy chicken thighs cooked in a rich and perfectly seasoned cheesy cream sauce. Not only that, but these chicken thighs can be cooked in less than 30 minutes. Enjoy.

PREPARATION TIME: 10 MINUTES
COOKING TIME: 16 MINUTES
PER SERVING (4): KCAL: 272; FAT: 9G; CARBS: 37G; PROTEIN: 23G; SUGARS: 7G; FIBRE: 12G.

INGRENKEDIENTS:

- 600g chicken thighs
- 20ml extra virgin olive oil
- 30g butter
- 2 garlic cloves, minced
- 120g sun-dried tomatoes
- 20g fresh thyme, chopped
- 120ml heavy cream
- 175ml chicken stock
- 60g Parmesan cheese, grated
- 1 teaspoon crushed red pepper flakes
- 1 teaspoon sea salt
- 1 teaspoon black pepper
- 30g fresh basil, chopped

INSTRUCTIONS:

Step 1: Preheat your air fryer to 180°C.

Step 2: Drizzle the chicken thighs with olive oil and season with sea salt and pepper; rub well and place the chicken in the air fryer basket. Cook for about 4 minutes per side or until golden brown.

Step 3: Meanwhile, heat the butter in a skillet over medium heat and sauté the garlic, sun-dried tomatoes, thyme, and pepper flakes for about 3 minutes.

Step 4: Stir in the chicken stock, heavy cream, Parmesan cheese, sea salt, and pepper, and cook for 2 minutes.

Step 5: Transfer the cream mixture to a baking dish that fits into your air fryer and place the chicken on top.

Step 6: Place in the air fryer and cook at 160°C for 12 minutes.

Step 7: Serve the casserole topped with chopped basil.

2. Air Fryer Duck Breasts With Lemon-Butter Sauce

Enjoy making this fancy, super-tasty, and one of the best and easiest duck recipes you'll make. With a mouthwatering lemon-butter sauce, you'll find yourself making this dish over and over again.

PREPARATION TIME: 12 HOURS
COOKING TIME: 15 MINUTES
PER SERVING (2): KCAL: 475; FAT: 12G; CARBS: 10G; PROTEIN: 48G; SUGARS: 7G; FIBRE: 3G.

INGREDIENTS:

- 250g duck breasts
- 240ml white wine
- 20g butter
- 120ml fresh lemon juice
- 6 tarragon sprigs
- 2 garlic cloves, minced
- 60ml soy sauce
- ½ teaspoon sea salt
- ½ teaspoon black pepper

NSTRUCTIONS:

Step 1: Preheat your air fryer to 180°C.

Step 2: In a large bowl, mix together the duck breasts, minced garlic, soy sauce, white wine, tarragon, sea salt, and pepper; toss to combine well, then store in the fridge for at least 12 hours. The longer it stays in the fridge, the better.

Step 3: Transfer the marinated duck, reserving the marinade, in the air fryer basket and cook for about 10 minutes. Flip over the duck breasts and continue cooking for another 10 minutes.

Step 4: Meanwhile, add the marinade to a skillet and stir in the fresh lemon juice and butter. Bring the mixture to a gentle boil over medium-high heat, then lower the heat to medium. Simmer for 5 minutes or until the sauce is thickened.

Step 5: Remove from the heat and set side.

Step 6: Divide the cooked duck breasts among serving plates and drizzle with the sauce. Serve right away!

3. Lime Duck With Shallots and Butter Sauce

Enjoy this juicy air-fried lime duck that's ready in only 20 minutes. The chicken stock, lime, and honey balance the flavours of the sauce with a hint of orange.

PREPARATION TIME: 10 MINUTES
COOKING TIME: 20 MINUTES
PER SERVING (4): KCAL: 228; FAT: 11G; CARBS: 20G; PROTEIN: 12G; SUGARS: 11G; FIBRE: 2G.

INGRENKEDIENTS:

- 2 boneless duck breasts, cut in halves
- 30ml fresh lime juice
- 600ml chicken stock
- 50g butter
- 240g shallot, chopped
- 1 tablespoon raw honey
- 350ml fresh orange juice
- ½ teaspoon sea salt
- ½ teaspoon black pepper

INSTRUCTIONS:

Step 1: Preheat your air fryer to 180°C.

Step 2: Drizzle duck with fresh lime juice and season with sea salt and pepper.

Step 3: Add the air fryer basket and cook for about 10 minutes or until golden brown on the outside.

Step 4: Meanwhile, melt butter in a skillet over medium heat and sauté the shallots for about 3 minutes.

Step 5: Stir in the stock and cook for 1 minute.

Step 6: Stir in the orange juice, raw honey, sea salt, and pepper. Cook for about 3 minutes.

Step 7: Divide the cooked duck on serving plates and drizzle with the sauce. Enjoy!

4. Turkey, Mushroom, and Pea Casserole

This creamy turkey, mushroom, and pea casserole is not only super delicious but a very versatile comfort food. It can be eaten as is or served alongside toast, noodles, cornbread, puff pastry, or biscuits.

PREPARATION TIME: 10 MINUTES
COOKING TIME: 20 MINUTES
PER SERVING (4): KCAL: 371; FAT: 11G; CARBS: 16G; PROTEIN: 7G; SUGARS: 2G; FIBRE: 9G.

INGREDIENTS:

- 30ml extra virgin olive oil
- 240g red onion, chopped
- 900g skinless, boneless turkey breasts, diced
- 120g peas
- 240g celery stalk, chopped
- ½ teaspoon sea salt
- ½ teaspoon black pepper
- 240ml cream of mushroom soup
- 240ml chicken stock

INSTRUCTIONS:

Step 1: Preheat your air fryer to 180°C.

Step 2: Heat olive oil in a pan that fits into your air fryer and sauté the onion and celery for about 5 minutes or until tender.

Step 3: Stir in the turkey, peas, sea salt, pepper, mushroom soup, and chicken stock, and place the pan in the air fryer.

Step 4: Cook for 15 minutes.

Step 5: Divide the turkey casserole among serving plates and serve right away!

5. Air-Fried Chicken Thighs

Juicy chicken thighs that are crispy skinned, seasoned to perfection, and served with a sweet and sour sauce. These air-fried chicken thighs will have everyone at the dinner table asking for more.

PREPARATION TIME: 10 MINUTES
COOKING TIME: 20 MINUTES
PER SERVING (6): KCAL: 321; FAT: 8G; CARBS: 36G; PROTEIN: 24G; SUGARS: 12G; FIBRE: 12G.

INGRENKEDIENTS:

- 1.25kg chicken thighs
- 240g fresh green onions, chopped
- ½ teaspoon brown sugar
- 20ml soy sauce
- 1 teaspoon white vinegar
- 20ml sherry wine
- 30ml sesame oil
- ½ teaspoon sea salt
- ½ teaspoon black pepper

INSTRUCTIONS:

Step 1: Preheat your air fryer to 180°C.

Step 2: Rub the chicken with half of the sesame oil and season with sea salt and pepper.

Step 3: Meanwhile, heat the remaining oil in a skillet over medium heat and stir in the green onions, brown sugar, soy sauce, vinegar, and sherry wine. Cook for 10 minutes or until the sauce is thickened.

Step 4: Remove the chicken from the air fryer and serve on plates drizzled with the sauce.

6. Air Fryer Duck With Veggies

This one-pot duck and veggies recipe is not only great for saving time, but the taste is out of this world. The flavours from the veggies, white wine, chicken stock, and duck blend perfectly to give a delicious and convenient one-pot dinner.

PREPARATION TIME: 10 MINUTES
COOKING TIME: 20 MINUTES
PER SERVING (8): KCAL: 200; FAT: 10G; CARBS: 20G; PROTEIN: 22G; SUGARS: 7G; FIBRE: 8G.

INGREDIENTS:

- 2kg duck, diced
- 2 carrots, chopped
- 3 cucumbers, chopped
- 1 tablespoon fresh ginger, grated
- 240ml chicken stock
- 50ml white wine
- ½ teaspoon sea salt
- ½ teaspoon black pepper

NSTRUCTIONS:

Step 1: Preheat your air fryer to 180°C.

Step 2: Combine all the ingredients in a pan that fits into your air fryer.

Step 3: Place the pan in the air fryer and cook for about 20 minutes or until the veggies are tender.

Step 4: Divide the duck and veggies among serving plates and serve right away.

7. Air Fryer Pepperoni Chicken

Craving pizza but looking for a healthier alternative without compromising on taste? This air fryer pepperoni chicken recipe is exactly what you need! With the chicken as the base, you will enjoy this high protein pepperoni chicken that tastes absolutely amazing!

PREPARATION TIME: 10 MINUTES
COOKING TIME: 22 MINUTES
PER SERVING (6): KCAL: 320; FAT: 10G; CARBS: 23G; PROTEIN: 27G; SUGARS: 1G; FIBRE: 16G.

INGRENKEDIENTS:

- 4 chicken breasts, skinless and boneless
- 20ml extra virgin olive oil
- 1 teaspoon dried oregano
- 500g tomato purée
- 150g mozzarella cheese, sliced
- 100g pepperoni, sliced
- 1 teaspoon garlic powder
- ½ teaspoon sea salt
- ½ teaspoon black pepper

INSTRUCTIONS:

Step 1: Preheat your air fryer to 180°C.

Step 2: Add the chicken to a large bowl, and stir in the oregano, garlic powder, sea salt, and pepper until the chicken is well coated.

Step 3: Place the chicken in the air fryer basket and cook for about 6 minutes.

Step 4: Transfer the cooked chicken to a pan that fits in your air fryer.

Step 5: Place the cheese slices on top of the chicken and spread with tomato purée. Arrange the pepperoni slices on top and return to the air fryer.

Step 6: Cook for 15 minutes, then remove from the air fryer.

Step 7: Serve right away!

8. Air Fryer Coconut Chicken

Coconut, chicken, and garlic is a marriage made in culinary heaven! Juicy and flavourful, this is sure to be a hit at your dinner table.

PREPARATION TIME: 2 HOURS
COOKING TIME: 25 MINUTES
PER SERVING (4): KCAL: 300; FAT: 4G; CARBS: 22G; PROTEIN: 20G; SUGARS: 3G; FIBRE: 12G.

INGREDIENTS:

- 4 chicken breasts, skinless and boneless
- 250g green onions, chopped
- 30g garlic, minced
- 60ml coconut cream
- 20g turmeric powder
- ½ teaspoon sea salt
- ½ teaspoon pepper

INSTRUCTIONS:

Step 1: Preheat your air fryer to 190°C.

Step 2: Mix everything in a pan that fits into your fryer.

Step 3: Cook in the air fryer for about 25 minutes.

Step 4: To serve, divide the chicken along with the sauce among serving plates, and serve with a salad on the side. Enjoy!

9. Lemon and Herb Air Fryer Chicken

Crispy and juicy air fryer chicken breasts are an easy dinner. This recipe uses boneless, skin-on chicken breasts with a lemon-herb mix that's cooked until crisp and golden on the outside and juicy on the inside.

PREPARATION TIME: 30 MINUTES
COOKING TIME: 20 MINUTES
PER SERVING (4): KCAL: 390; FAT: 10G; CARBS: 22G; PROTEIN: 20G; SUGARS: 2G; FIBRE: 5G.

INGRENKEDIENTS:

- 4 boneless, skin-on chicken breasts
- 120ml fresh lemon juice
- 30ml extra virgin olive oil
- 1 teaspoon dried rosemary
- 1 teaspoon dried thyme
- 1 teaspoon onion powder
- 1 teaspoon garlic powder
- ½ teaspoon sea salt
- ½ teaspoon black pepper

INSTRUCTIONS:

Step 1: Preheat your air fryer to 180°C and grease the air fryer basket.

Step 2: In a large bowl, mix the fresh lemon juice, olive oil, rosemary, thyme, onion powder, garlic powder, sea salt, and pepper until well blended.

Step 3: Rub the lemon-herb mix over the chicken breasts and transfer to a greased air fryer basket.

Step 4: Cook for 10 minutes per side or until golden brown.

10. Chicken, Peas, and Rice Casserole

This air fryer chicken, peas, and chicken casserole is the ultimate comfort food! It's easy to make, with versatile ingredients that you can switch up depending on your preference. Enjoy this easy dinner!

PREPARATION TIME: 10 MINUTES
COOKING TIME: 40 MINUTES
PER SERVING (4): KCAL: 313; FAT: 12G; CARBS: 27G; PROTEIN: 44G; SUGARS: 9G; FIBRE: 14G.

INGREDIENTS:

- 240g rice
- 470g frozen peas
- 500g boneless, skinless chicken breasts, diced
- 20ml extra virgin olive oil
- 30g butter
- 3 garlic cloves, minced
- 240g red onion, chopped
- 240ml chicken stock
- 60ml heavy cream
- 120ml white wine
- 350g Parmesan cheese, grated
- 60g parsley, chopped
- ½ teaspoon sea salt
- ½ teaspoon black pepper

NSTRUCTIONS:

Step 1: Combine rice with 500ml of water in a pot and stir in the sea salt. Bring to a boil on high heat. Lower the heat to medium-low and simmer for about 20 minutes or until tender.

Step 2: Meanwhile, preheat your air fryer to 180°C.

Step 3: Drizzle the chicken breasts with olive oil and season with sea salt and pepper; rub well and place the chicken in the air fryer basket. Cook for about 6 minutes per side or until golden brown. Transfer to a baking dish that fits into your air fryer. Add in the rice and peas and set aside.

Step 4: Heat the butter in a pan over medium heat until it melts, then sauté the red onions for about 4 minutes or until the onion is tender. Add in the garlic and stir for 1 minute. Stir in the chicken stock, wine, heavy cream, sea salt, and pepper, and cook for about 9 minutes.

Step 5: Pour the cream mixture over the chicken mix, and sprinkle with Parmesan cheese and chopped parsley.

Step 6: Place the dish in the air fryer and cook for 10 minutes at 210°C. Serve hot.

11. Air Fryer Duck Breasts With Orange and Red Wine Sauce

Juicy and full of flavour, these air fryer duck breasts with orange and red wine sauce is an elegant dish that is perfect for a date night or a night where you are entertaining. The pumpkin pie spice in the sauce adds some delicious uniqueness to this recipe. It pairs really well with creamy potato gratin or crispy potatoes with a side of veggies. Enjoy!

PREPARATION TIME: 10 MINUTES
COOKING TIME: 35 MINUTES
PER SERVING (4): KCAL: 300; FAT: 8G; CARBS: 24G; PROTEIN: 11G; SUGARS: 10G; FIBRE: 12G.

INGRENKEDIENTS:

- 2 duck breasts, cut into halves
- 30g butter
- 30ml olive oil
- 2 teaspoons pumpkin pie spice
- 30ml sherry vinegar
- 120g raw honey
- 800ml red wine
- 500ml orange juice
- 500ml chicken stock
- ½ teaspoon sea salt
- ½ teaspoon black pepper

INSTRUCTIONS:

Step 1: Preheat your air fryer to 180°C.

Step 2: Sprinkle the duck breasts with sea salt and rub with extra virgin olive oil.

Step 3: Place the duck breasts in the air fryer basket and cook for about 8 minutes per side or until golden brown on the outside.

Step 4: Meanwhile, add the fresh orange juice and raw honey to a skillet and cook over medium heat for about 10 minutes, stirring throughout.

Step 5: Stir in the chicken stock, vinegar, wine, butter, and pie spice, and cook for another 10 minutes. Then remove from the heat.

Step 6: To serve, divide the duck on serving plates and drizzle with the orange-wine sauce. Enjoy!

12. Duck Breast With Shallot-Butter Sauce

Perfectly cooked medium-rare duck breast is a tasty delight. Juicy, tender, rosy, and super flavourful, this recipe is simple and topped with a tasty pan sauce that's made by sweating shallots in the pan and deglazing with cooking wine and chicken stock. You will enjoy every bite!

PREPARATION TIME: 10 MINUTES
COOKING TIME: 20 MINUTES
PER SERVING (4): KCAL: 246; FAT: 12G; CARBS: 22G; PROTEIN: 3G; SUGARS: 12G; FIBRE: 4G.

INGREDIENTS:

- 2 duck breasts, cut into halves
- 20ml extra virgin olive oil
- 240g shallot, chopped
- 50g butter
- 240ml chicken stock
- ½ teaspoon sweet paprika
- ½ teaspoon garlic powder
- ½ teaspoon thyme, chopped
- 20g white flour
- 120ml cooking wine
- ½ teaspoon sea salt
- ½ teaspoon black pepper

INSTRUCTIONS:

Step 1: Preheat your air fryer to 180°C.

Step 2: Add half of the butter to a skillet and melt over medium heat; stir in the sea salt and pepper until well combined.

Step 3: Rub the duck breasts with the butter mix, then place into the air fryer basket.

Step 4: Cook for 5 minutes per side or until the duck is golden brown.

Step 5: Set a skillet over medium heat, and add the in olive oil and the remaining butter.

Step 6: Stir the chopped shallots into the butter mix and cook for 2 minutes. Then stir in the paprika, garlic powder, thyme, wine, sea salt, pepper, and chicken stock.

Step 7: Cook for about 8 minutes, then stir in the flour.

Step 8: Cook for about 3 minutes or until the sauce thickens.

Step 9: Serve the duck breasts on serving plates drizzled with the sauce.

13. Air Fryer Lemon Chicken

This quick air fryer lemon pepper chicken recipe is going to be your go-to chicken breast recipe. They're juicy, tender, delicious, and packed full of flavour, and the best part is they're ready in only 30 minutes!

PREPARATION TIME: 10 MINUTES
COOKING TIME: 30 MINUTES
PER SERVING (6): KCAL: 334; FAT: 24G; CARBS: 26G; PROTEIN: 20G; SUGARS: 2G; FIBRE: 12G.

INGRENKEDIENTS:

- • 6 chicken breasts
- • 60ml fresh lemon juice
- • 1 tablespoon fresh lemon zest
- • 20ml extra virgin olive oil
- • ½ teaspoon sea salt
- • ½ teaspoon black pepper

INSTRUCTIONS:

Step 1: Preheat your oven to 180°C.

Step 2: In a small bowl, mix together the fresh lemon juice, lemon zest, olive oil, sea salt, and pepper until well combined. Rub the mixture over the chicken breasts until well coated.

Step 3: Place the chicken in the air fryer basket and cook for 30 minutes, flipping the chicken breasts halfway. The chicken breasts should be cooked through and golden brown on the outside.

Step 4: Divide among serving plates and serve with your favourite green salad.

14. Air Fryer Chicken With Green Onions and Coconut Sauce

An easy weeknight curry-like recipe cooked in your air fryer. You simply add the ingredients in different stages and they all come together beautifully to create a flavourful dish in only 12 minutes!

PREPARATION TIME: 10 MINUTES
COOKING TIME: 12 MINUTES
PER SERVING (6): KCAL: 320; FAT: 13G; CARBS: 32G; PROTEIN: 23G; SUGARS: 6G; FIBRE: 13G.

INGREDIENTS:

- • 20ml extra virgin olive oil
- • 500g red onion, chopped
- • 1.25kg chicken breasts
- • 20ml fresh lime juice
- • 240ml chicken stock
- • 120ml coconut milk
- • 240g green onions, chopped
- • 2 teaspoons paprika
- • 1 teaspoon red pepper flakes
- • ½ teaspoon sea salt
- • ½ teaspoon black pepper

NSTRUCTIONS:

Step 1: Preheat your air fryer to 180°C.

Step 2: Heat the olive oil in a pan that fits in your air fryer. Add in the red onions and sauté for 4 minutes or until fragrant and tender.

Step 3: Stir in the fresh lime juice, paprika, red pepper flakes, green onions, coconut milk, chicken stock, sea salt, and pepper until well combined.

Step 4: Add in the chicken and toss to coat well.

Step 5: Place the basket in the air fryer and cook for about 12 minutes.

Step 6: Serve the chicken drizzled with the sauce.

15. Cheese-Crusted Chicken

This cheese-crusted chicken is a very easy and satisfying recipe that is moist, tender, coated in a cheesy mix, and cooked in the air fryer for perfect crispiness.

PREPARATION TIME: 10 MINUTES
COOKING TIME: 15 MINUTES
PER SERVING (4): KCAL: 400; FAT: 22G; CARBS: 32G; PROTEIN: 47G; SUGARS: 3G; FIBRE: 12G.

INGRENKEDIENTS:

- 4 bacon slices, sliced
- 120ml avocado oil
- 4 boneless, skinless chicken breasts
- 20ml water
- 1 egg
- 240g Parmesan cheese, grated
- ½ teaspoon garlic powder
- ½ teaspoon black pepper
- ½ teaspoon sea salt
- 240g Asiago cheese, grated

INSTRUCTIONS:

Step 1: Preheat your air fryer to 180°C.

Step 2: Add the bacon to a skillet and cook for about 10 minutes or until golden brown and crispy. Transfer to a plate and set aside.

Step 3: In a large bowl, stir together minced garlic, cheese, sea salt, and pepper until well combined.

Step 4: In a separate bowl, whisk together the egg and water until blended.

Step 5: Sprinkle the chicken with sea salt and black pepper, then dip into the egg wash. Dredge in the cheese mix until well coated, then place in the air fryer basket.

Step 6: Cook for about 15 minutes or until golden brown on the outside.

Step 7: To serve, divide the cooked chicken among serving plates and top with bacon and Asiago cheese. Enjoy!

16. Air Fryer Chicken With Green Onion Sauce

This air fryer chicken with creamy green onion sauce is such a comforting meal and perfect for winter or cold nights. Ready in about half an hour, you are going to enjoy this quick and deliciously flavoured dish.

PREPARATION TIME: 10 MINUTES
COOKING TIME: 26 MINUTES
PER SERVING (4): KCAL: 321; FAT: 12G; CARBS: 21G; PROTEIN: 20G; SUGARS: 11G; FIBRE: 7G.

INGREDIENTS:

- 10 chicken drumsticks
- 250g green onions, chopped
- 2 teaspoons fresh ginger root, grated
- 4 garlic cloves, minced
- 1 teaspoon butter, melted
- 240ml coconut milk
- 1 teaspoon Chinese five spice
- 50ml soy sauce
- 30ml fish sauce
- ½ teaspoon sea salt
- ½ teaspoon black pepper
- 60g fresh coriander, chopped
- 20ml fresh lime juice

NSTRUCTIONS:

Step 1: Preheat your air fryer to 180°C.

Step 2: Combine the green onions, garlic, ginger, Chinese five spice, fish sauce, soy sauce, butter, coconut milk, sea salt, and pepper in a food processor. Process until very smooth.

Step 3: Pour the green onion mix into a pan that fits into your air fryer and toss in the chicken until well coated.

Step 4: Transfer to the preheated air fryer and cook for 16 minutes. Remove the pan from the air fryer, stir to mix well, then return. Cook for another 10 minutes.

Step 5: To serve, divide the chicken among serving plates, top with chopped coriander, and drizzle with fresh lime juice. Enjoy!

17. Air Fryer Chicken Cacciatore

This Italian-inspired chicken dish is such a breeze to prepare. All you need to do is combine all the ingredients in your air fryer and it will be ready in 20 minutes. The rustic tomato sauce and the moist and tender chicken thighs pair really well with pasta, sautéed veg, or rice.

PREPARATION TIME: 10 MINUTES
COOKING TIME: 20 MINUTES
PER SERVING (4): KCAL: 300; FAT: 12G; CARBS: 20G; PROTEIN: 24G; SUGARS: 4G; FIBRE: 8G.

INGREDIENTS:

- 8 bone-in chicken drumsticks
- 1 yellow onion, chopped
- 120g black olives, pitted and sliced
- 800g canned tomatoes and juice, crushed
- 1 teaspoon garlic powder
- 1 teaspoon dried oregano
- 1 bay leaf
- ½ teaspoon sea salt
- ½ teaspoon black pepper

INSTRUCTIONS:

Step 1: Preheat your air fryer to 180°C.

Step 2: Combine everything in a dish that fits into your air fryer.

Step 3: Place the dish into the air fryer and cook for about 20 minutes.

Step 4: Divide among serving plates and serve. Enjoy!

18. Air Fryer Turkey With Vegetables

One of the simplest ways to make a great dinner is with air fryer turkey with vegetables. It's full of flavour and only takes 34 minutes!

PREPARATION TIME: 10 MINUTES
COOKING TIME: 34 MINUTES
PER SERVING (4): KCAL: 362; FAT: 12G; CARBS: 19G; PROTEIN: 23G; SUGARS: 1G; FIBRE: 16G.

INGREDIENTS:

- 30ml extra virgin olive oil
- 1kg turkey meat, diced
- 240ml chicken stock
- 1 red onion, chopped
- 1 celery stalk, chopped
- 3 garlic cloves, minced
- 1 carrot, chopped
- ½ teaspoon dried thyme
- ½ teaspoon dried sage
- ½ teaspoon dried rosemary
- 2 bay leaves
- ½ teaspoon sea salt
- ½ teaspoon black pepper

INSTRUCTIONS:

Step 1: Preheat your air fryer to 180°C.

Step 2: Mix half of the olive oil, thyme, rosemary, sage, sea salt, and pepper in a small bowl; rub the mixture over the turkey meat until well coated, and place in the preheated air fryer.

Step 3: Cook for 20 minutes, then remove from air fryer.

Step 4: Heat the remaining oil in a pan that fits into your air fryer and sauté the onion for 4 minutes. Stir in the garlic, bay leaves, stock, sea salt, and pepper. Cook for 3 minutes, then add in the turkey.

Step 5: Place the pan in the air fryer and cook for 14 minutes.

19. Air Fryer Chicken With Garlic Sauce

Air fryer chicken with garlic sauce is a crispy, moist, and tender dish made with a perfectly seasoned garlic sauce. A quick and tasty dinner that's ready in 20 minutes!

PREPARATION TIME: 10 MINUTES
COOKING TIME: 20 MINUTES
PER SERVING (4): KCAL: 227; FAT: 9G; CARBS: 24G; PROTEIN: 19G; SUGARS: 11G; FIBRE: 13G.

INGRENKEDIENTS:

- 20g butter, melted
- 20ml extra virgin olive oil
- 4 garlic cloves, chopped
- 4 chicken breasts
- 100ml chicken stock
- 60ml dry white wine
- 2 thyme sprigs
- 30g fresh parsley, chopped
- ½ teaspoon sea salt
- ½ teaspoon black pepper

INSTRUCTIONS:

Step 1: Preheat your oven to 180°C.

Step 2: Rub the chicken breasts with oil and sprinkle with sea salt and pepper.

Step 3: Place in the air fryer basket and cook for about 5 minutes per side. Transfer the chicken to a baking dish that fits into your air fryer.

Step 4: Add the garlic, butter, wine, stock, thyme, and parsley to the dish, and toss to mix well. Place the dish into the air fryer and cook for 15 minutes.

Step 5: To serve, divide the chicken breasts among serving plates and drizzle with the sauce. Enjoy!

20. Lemon Duck Breasts

Learn how to cook crisp and juicy duck breast with our lemon duck breast recipe. Crispy skin and tender flavourful meat will always be a win!

PREPARATION TIME: 10 MINUTES
COOKING TIME: 15 MINUTES
PER SERVING (4): KCAL: 200; FAT: 7G; CARBS: 11G; PROTEIN: 21G; SUGARS: 1G; FIBRE: 3G.

INGREDIENTS:

- 4 duck breasts, skinless and boneless
- 20ml extra virgin olive oil
- 4 garlic cloves, minced
- 50ml fresh lemon juice
- ½ teaspoon lemon pepper
- ½ teaspoon sea salt
- ½ teaspoon black pepper

INSTRUCTIONS:

Step 1: In a large bowl, mix together the fresh lemon juice, olive oil, garlic, lemon pepper, sea salt, and pepper until well blended. Toss in the duck breasts and marinate for about 30 minutes.

Step 2: Preheat your air fryer to 180°C.

Step 3: Transfer the duck breasts along with the marinade to a baking dish that fits into your air fryer.

Step 4: Place the dish in the air fryer and cook for 15 minutes.

Step 5: Serve hot.

21. Honey Duck Breasts

This honey duck breasts recipe is the perfect introduction to crisp and juicy duck cooked in a sweet and sour sauce. Feel free to add chillies if you like a little heat in your food.

PREPARATION TIME: 10 MINUTES
COOKING TIME: 22 MINUTES
PER SERVING (2): KCAL: 374; FAT: 11G; CARBS: 32G; PROTEIN: 22G; SUGARS: 14G; FIBRE: 13G.

INGRENKEDIENTS:

- 250g smoked duck breast, diced
- 1 teaspoon raw honey
- 1 teaspoon tomato purée
- 20g mustard
- 1 teaspoon apple cider vinegar

INSTRUCTIONS:

Step 1: Preheat your air fryer to 180°C.

Step 2: In a large bowl, whisk together the tomato purée, raw honey, vinegar, and mustard.

Step 3: Toss in the duck meat until well coated, then place in the air fryer basket.

Step 4: Cook for about 15 minutes.

Step 5: Remove the duck from the air fryer and baste with the honey mixture. Return to the air fryer and cook for another 6 minutes.

Step 6: Serve.

22. Air Fryer Chicken Thighs and Potatoes

This air fryer chicken thighs and potatoes is extremely delicious and a fun, quick, and easy dinner perfect for weeknights or when you are pressed for time. The bone-in chicken thighs, potatoes, and herbs combine really well for a flavourful dish that's ready in only half an hour.

PREPARATION TIME: 10 MINUTES
COOKING TIME: 30 MINUTES
PER SERVING (4): KCAL: 364; FAT: 14G; CARBS: 21G; PROTEIN: 34G; SUGARS: 2G; FIBRE: 13G.

INGREDIENTS:

- 30ml extra virgin olive oil
- 8 chicken thighs
- 500g potatoes, halved
- 1 red onion, chopped
- 2 garlic cloves, minced
- ½ teaspoon paprika
- 2 teaspoons fresh thyme, chopped
- 2 teaspoons dried rosemary
- 2 teaspoons dried oregano
- ½ teaspoon sea salt
- ½ teaspoon black pepper

INSTRUCTIONS:

Step 1: Preheat your air fryer to 200°C.

Step 2: Mix all the ingredients in a bowl until well combined; spread into a baking dish that fits into your air fryer.

Step 3: Place the baking dish into the air fryer and cook for 30 minutes, shaking halfway.

Step 4: Serve hot. Enjoy!

23. Lemon Chicken With Capers

Buttery and tangy with garlic infusion, this lemon chicken with capers is super tasty and easy to make. Moist and tender with crispy skin, you will enjoy every delicious bite of this meal.

PREPARATION TIME: 10 MINUTES
COOKING TIME: 20 MINUTES
PER SERVING (2): KCAL: 300; FAT: 9G; CARBS: 17G; PROTEIN: 23G; SUGARS: 3G; FIBRE: 10G.

INGRENKEDIENTS:

*   4 chicken thighs
*   3 tablespoons capers
*   4 garlic cloves, minced
*   50g butter, melted
*   ½ teaspoon sea salt
*   ½ teaspoon black pepper
*   120ml chicken stock
*   1 lemon, sliced
*   4 green onions, chopped

INSTRUCTIONS:

Step 1: Preheat your air fryer to 180°C.

Step 2: Smear butter over the chicken, and season with sea salt and pepper; place in a baking dish that fits into your air fryer.

Step 3: Add the chicken stock, garlic, capers, and lemon slices on top of the chicken, and place the dish into the air fryer.

Step 4: Cook for 20 minutes, stirring halfway.

Step 5: To serve, divide among serving plates and top with the chopped green onions. Enjoy!

24. Air Fryer Chicken With Creamy Mushrooms

This one-pot creamy chicken dish is savoury, delicious, and enough to serve the whole family. All you need is 40 minutes from start to finish. Be prepared for second helpings because it's that good!

PREPARATION TIME: 10 MINUTES
COOKING TIME: 30 MINUTES
PER SERVING (8): KCAL: 340; FAT: 10G; CARBS: 27G; PROTEIN: 33G; SUGARS: 5G; FIBRE: 13G.

INGREDIENTS:

*   60g butter, melted
*   8 chicken thighs
*   250g red onion, chopped
*   3 garlic cloves, minced
*   300g cremini mushrooms, cut into halves
*   60ml heavy cream
*   250ml chicken stock
*   ½ teaspoon dried oregano
*   ½ teaspoon dried thyme
*   ½ teaspoon dried basil
*   60g Parmesan cheese, grated
*   1 tablespoon mustard
*   ½ teaspoon each of sea salt and black pepper

NSTRUCTIONS:

Step 1: Preheat your air fryer to 180°C.

Step 2: Rub the chicken with half of the butter and sprinkle with sea salt and pepper.

Step 3: Place the chicken in the air fryer basket and cook for 5 minutes.

Step 4: Transfer the chicken to a bowl and set aside.

Step 5: Meanwhile, heat the remaining butter in a skillet and stir in the red onions for 4 minutes or until tender. Stir in the garlic and mushrooms and cook for 5 minutes.

Step 6: Stir in the basil, thyme, oregano, stock, sea salt, and pepper until well combined, and transfer to a baking dish that fits into your air fryer.

Step 7: Add the chicken to the dish and toss to coat well. Place the baking dish in the air fryer and cook for 20 minutes.

Step 8: Remove the dish from the air fryer and stir in the heavy cream, mustard, and Parmesan cheese. Return to the air fryer and cook for 5 minutes.

Step 9: Divide the casserole among serving plates and serve right away.

25. Simple Air-Fried Duck Breasts

These simple air-fried duck breasts make a great dinner for those nights when you want to make something a bit different. It only cooks in 20 minutes and comes out deliciously succulent and flavourful with a beautifully crispy skin.

PREPARATION TIME: 10 MINUTES
COOKING TIME: 20 MINUTES
PER SERVING (6): KCAL: 336; FAT: 12G; CARBS: 25G; PROTEIN: 33G; SUGARS: 17G; FIBRE: 1G.

INGRENKEDIENTS:

- 6 boneless duck breasts
- 1 teaspoon sesame oil
- 4 ginger slices
- 60ml soy sauce
- 60ml hoisin sauce
- 2 teaspoons Chinese five spice
- 600ml chicken stock
- 2 tablespoons raw honey
- ½ teaspoon sea salt
- ½ teaspoon black pepper

INSTRUCTIONS:

Step 1: Preheat your air fryer to 200°C.

Step 2: In a large bowl, mix together the duck breasts, Chinese five spice, raw honey, soy sauce, sea salt, and pepper. Set aside.

Step 3: Heat the sesame oil in a skillet, and stir in the ginger and hoisin sauce. Cook for 3 minutes, then remove from the heat.

Step 4: Place the duck breasts along with the marinade in a baking dish that fits into your air fryer and cook in the preheated air fryer for 15 minutes.

Step 5: Divide the cooked duck among serving plates and drizzle with hoisin sauce.

26. Turkey With Lime and Green Onion Sauce

There's something about turkey and lime that makes it a perfect combination. Add in some fresh herbs, honey, olive oil, and red wine, and you've got yourself a perfect dinner!

PREPARATION TIME: 30 MINUTES
COOKING TIME: 25 MINUTES
PER SERVING (6): KCAL: 354; FAT: 10G; CARBS: 22G; PROTEIN: 17G; SUGARS: 14G; FIBRE: 9G.

INGREDIENTS:

- 800g turkey breasts, diced
- 200g fresh parsley, chopped
- 1 tablespoon raw honey
- 200g green onions, chopped
- 120ml olive oil
- 1 teaspoon dried oregano
- 60ml red wine
- 4 garlic cloves
- ½ teaspoon sea salt
- 60ml fresh lime juice

INSTRUCTIONS:

Step 1: Combine the green onions, parsley, olive oil, garlic, oregano, wine, raw honey, and sea salt in a food processor. Process until very smooth.

Step 2: Mix in the turkey and toss until well coated.

Step 3: Place in the fridge and marinate for at least 30 minutes.

Step 4: Preheat your air fryer to 180°C.

Step 5: Drain the turkey from the marinade and place in the air fryer basket. Cook for 25 minutes, flipping the turkey once.

Step 6: Meanwhile, add the marinade to a skillet and cook over medium heat for about 8 minutes or until thickened. Remove from the heat and stir in the fresh lime juice.

Step 7: Divide the cooked turkey among serving plates and drizzle each with the sauce.

27. Air Fryer Turkey and Lentils Casserole

This air-fried turkey and lentils casserole is such a great, filling, and super-tasty dish. It'll shock you how fast it goes!

PREPARATION TIME: 10 MINUTES
COOKING TIME: 1 HOUR
PER SERVING (8): KCAL: 344; FAT: 11G; CARBS: 34G; PROTEIN: 33G; SUGARS: 14G; FIBRE: 12G.

INGREKEDIENTS:
_____

- 1kg turkey skinless, boneless breasts, diced
- 30ml olive oil
- 400g green lentils
- 1 red onion, chopped
- 500g sweetcorn
- 400g cheddar cheese, grated
- 750ml chicken stock
- 5 garlic cloves, minced
- 2 red bell peppers, chopped
- 400g canned tomatoes, chopped
- 30g jalapeno pepper, chopped
- 3 teaspoons ground cumin
- 3 teaspoons garlic powder
- 200g coriander, chopped
- ½ teaspoon sea salt
- ½ teaspoon cayenne pepper

INSTRUCTIONS:
_____

Step 1: Add the chicken stock to a pot and stir in the sea salt and lentils. Bring to a rolling boil over high heat. Lower the heat and simmer for 35 minutes or until the lentils are tender.

Step 2: Preheat your air fryer to 180°C.

Step 3: Drizzle the turkey with olive oil and sprinkle with cumin, cayenne pepper, and sea salt. Place in the air fryer basket and cook for 6 minutes per side.

Step 4: Transfer the cooked turkey to a pan that fits into your air fryer, and add in the tomatoes, bell peppers, garlic, onion, cumin, cayenne pepper, and sea salt.

Step 5: Add the cooked lentils and sweetcorn to the turkey mix and sprinkle with grated cheese. Cook in the air fryer for 25 minutes or until the cheese is melted.

Step 6: Divide among serving plates and top with chopped coriander. Enjoy!

28. Simple Air Fryer Turkey Breasts

These simple air fryer turkey breasts come out so juicy, moist, and beautifully cooked with a rich brown and crispy skin. And what's more, they cook in a fraction of the time it would take in an oven.

PREPARATION TIME: 5 MINUTES
COOKING TIME: 55 MINUTES
PER SERVING (10): KCAL: 226; FAT: 10G; CARBS: 4G; PROTEIN: 33G; SUGARS: 1G; FIBRE: 0.5G.

INGREDIENTS:
_____

- 2kg turkey breasts
- 50g butter, melted
- 50ml fresh lemon juice
- 1 teaspoon onion powder
- 1 teaspoon paprika
- 1 teaspoon sea salt

INSTRUCTIONS:
_____

Step 1: Preheat your air fryer to 180°C.

Step 2: In a small bowl, mix the fresh lemon juice, melted butter, onion powder, paprika, sea salt, and pepper until well combined.

Step 3: Smear the lemon mix onto the turkey meat and place it in the air fryer basket.

Step 4: Cook for 20 minutes, then flip it over. Continue cooking for another 15 minutes.

Step 5: Remove the turkey from the air fryer and let it rest for at least 10 minutes. Slice and serve.

29. Lime Turkey Breasts

Buttery and infused with garlic, paprika, lime, sea salt, and black pepper flavours, these lime turkey breasts are tender and juicy with a crispy golden skin and perfect for a special weeknight dinner. Enjoy!

PREPARATION TIME: 10 MINUTES
COOKING TIME: 30 MINUTES
PER SERVING (4): KCAL: 539; FAT: 10G; CARBS: 5G; PROTEIN: 67G; SUGARS: 1G; FIBRE: 1G.

INGRENKEDIENTS:

*   2kg bone-in turkey breasts
*   100ml fresh lime juice
*   30ml extra virgin olive oil
*   50g butter, melted
*   1 teaspoon garlic powder
*   1 teaspoon paprika
*   ½ teaspoon sea salt
*   ½ teaspoon black pepper

INSTRUCTIONS:

Step 1: Preheat your air fryer to 180°C.

Step 2: In a small bowl, mix together the fresh lime juice, melted butter, olive oil, garlic powder, paprika, sea salt, and pepper until well combined.

Step 3: Smear the lime mix onto the turkey meat and place it in the air fryer basket.

Step 4: Cook for 20 minutes, then flip it over. Continue cooking for another 15 minutes.

Step 5: Remove the turkey from the air fryer and let it rest for at least 10 minutes. Slice and serve.

30. Delicious Air-Fried Duck Breasts

These delicious air-fried duck breasts are aptly named. The heavy cream seals and infuses more moisture into the duck breasts, giving you moist, juicy, and tender meat with a great fusion of flavours and crispy golden skin. Serve with roasted or mashed potatoes with a side of veggies.

PREPARATION TIME: 10 MINUTES
COOKING TIME: 35 MINUTES
PER SERVING (4): KCAL: 400; FAT: 12G; CARBS: 29G; PROTEIN: 28G; SUGARS: 12G; FIBRE: 22G.

INGREDIENTS:

*   2 duck breasts
*   20ml extra virgin olive oil
*   50ml heavy cream
*   20g garlic, minced
*   200g white wine
*   1 tablespoon raw honey
*   ½ teaspoon sea salt
*   ½ teaspoon black pepper

NSTRUCTIONS:

Step 1: Preheat your air fryer to 180°C.

Step 2: In a small bowl, mix together the fresh raw honey, wine, heavy cream, olive oil, garlic, sea salt, and pepper until well combined.

Step 3: Smear the cream mix onto the duck breasts and place it in the air fryer basket.

Step 4: Cook for 20 minutes, then flip it over. Continue cooking for another 15 minutes.

Step 5: Remove the duck breasts from the air fryer and let them rest for at least 10 minutes. Slice and serve.

FISH AND SEAFOOD

Don't Forget To Get The Color Images FREE!
Simply Scan The QR Code Below!

Hello! Please scan the QR code below to access your promised bonus of all our recipes with full colored photos & beautiful designs! It is the best we could do to keep the book as cheap as possible while providing the best value!

Also, once downloaded you can take the PDF with you digitally wherever you go- meaning you can cook these recipes wherever an Air Fryer is present!

STEP BY STEP Guide-

1. *Open Your Phones (Or Any Device You Want The Book On) Back Camera. The Back Camera Is The One You use as if you are taking a picture of someone.*

2. *Simply point your Camera at the QR code and 'tap' the QR code with your finger to focus the camera.*

3. *A link / pop up will appear. Simply tap that (and make sure you have internet connection) and the FREE PDF containing all of the colored images should appear.*

4. *If You Click On The File And It Says 'The File Is Too Big To Preview' Simply click 'Download' and it will download the full book onto your phone!*

5. *Now you have access to these FOREVER. Simply 'Bookmark' The tab it opened on, or download the document and take wherever you want.*

6. *Repeat this on any device you want it on!*

Any Issues / Feedback / Troubleshooting please email:
anthonypublishing123@gmail.com *and our customer service team will help you! We want to make sure you have the BEST experience with our books!*

1. Air-Fried Cod With Peas

Cod fillets are generously coated with a blend of garlic, parsley, paprika, garlic, sea salt, pepper, oregano, and wine, and they are air fried until flaky and golden. Served with peas and garlic sauce, this air-fried cod recipe is simple, tasty, and healthy.

PREPARATION TIME: 10 MINUTES

COOKING TIME: 10 MINUTES

PER SERVING (4): KCAL: 261; FAT: 7G; CARBS: 20G; PROTEIN: 22G; SUGARS: 7G; FIBRE: 12G.

INGRENKEDIENTS:

- 4 boneless cod fillets
- 2 garlic cloves, minced
- 500g peas
- ½ teaspoon sweet paprika
- ½ teaspoon dried oregano
- 60ml wine
- ¼ teaspoon sea salt
- ¼ teaspoon black pepper
- 30g parsley, chopped

INSTRUCTIONS:

Step 1: In a food processor, process the chopped parsley, garlic, paprika, oregano, wine, sea salt, and pepper until very smooth.

Step 2: Rub the cod fillets with half the garlic mix until well coated.

Step 3: Place the fish in the air fryer basket and cook at 180°C for 10 minutes.

Step 4: In the meantime, add the peas, salt, and water to a pot, and bring to a gentle boil. Lower the heat to medium and cook for 10 minutes or until tender; then drain.

Step 5: Add the remaining garlic mix to a skillet and cook for 5 minutes.

Step 6: Divide the cooked peas among serving plates and top each serving with the cod fillets. Drizzle with the garlic sauce. Enjoy!

2. Air-Fried Trout in Lemon-Chive Butter Sauce

This air-fried trout in lemon-chive butter sauce is an awesome recipe that will make your mouth water when you take a bite of these fillets. The air fryer cooks the fish to flaky perfection, and it only takes 10 minutes!

PREPARATION TIME: 10 MINUTES

COOKING TIME: 10 MINUTES

PER SERVING (4): KCAL: 315; FAT: 12G; CARBS: 27G; PROTEIN: 24G; SUGARS: 3G; FIBRE: 9G.

INGREDIENTS:

- 4 boneless trout fillets
- 2 tablespoons extra virgin olive oil
- ¼ teaspoon sea salt
- ¼ teaspoon black pepper
- 90g butter
- 250g chives
- 60ml fresh lemon juice
- 30g lemon zest, grated

NSTRUCTIONS:

Step 1: Drizzle olive oil over the trout fillets and season with sea salt and pepper; rub well and place in the air fryer basket.

Step 2: Cook at 180°C for 10 minutes, flipping halfway.

Step 3: In the meantime, heat butter in a skillet over medium heat and stir in the chives, fresh lemon juice, lemon zest, sea salt, and pepper; cook for 2 minutes, then remove from the heat.

Step 4: Divide the trout fillets among serving plates and drizzle with lemon-chive butter sauce. Enjoy!

3. Coconut Salmon Casserole

Quick, very easy, and loaded with creamy and cheesy goodness, this air fryer coconut salmon casserole is tasty, highly nutritious, and ready in only 10 minutes!

PREPARATION TIME: 10 MINUTES
COOKING TIME: 10 MINUTES
PER SERVING (4): KCAL: 214; FAT: 16G; CARBS: 17G; PROTEIN: 21G; SUGARS: 1G; FIBRE: 11G.

INGRENKEDIENTS:

- 4 boneless salmon fillets
- 20ml olive oil
- 80g cheddar cheese, grated
- 20g mustard
- 120ml coconut cream
- ¼ teaspoon sea salt
- ¼ teaspoon black pepper

INSTRUCTIONS:

Step 1: Drizzle olive oil over the salmon fillets and season with sea salt and pepper; rub well and place in a baking dish that fits into your air fryer.

Step 2: In a small bowl, whisk together the mustard, cheddar cheese, coconut cream, sea salt, and pepper until well combined; pour over the fish in the baking dish and place in the air fryer.

Step 3: Cook at 180°C for 10 minutes.

Step 4: Divide the fish casserole among serving plates and serve.

4. Lime Salmon With Healthy Avocado Salad

Fresh, healthy, delicious, and screaming of natural, this lime salmon is cooked beautifully in the air fryer and is ready to serve in 25 minutes alongside a beautiful pairing of avocado salad. Enjoy!

PREPARATION TIME: 15 MINUTES
COOKING TIME: 10 MINUTES
PER SERVING (8): KCAL: 415; FAT: 36G; CARBS: 12G; PROTEIN: 22G; SUGARS: 6G; FIBRE: 9G.

INGREDIENTS:

- 1 tablespoon extra virgin olive oil
- 500g lettuce, chopped
- 250g rocket
- 250g cucumber, diced
- 250g tomato, diced
- 250g red onion, chopped
- 2 avocados, diced
- 250g toasted walnuts, chopped
- 20ml balsamic vinegar
- 1 teaspoon extra virgin olive oil
- 800g salmon fillet
- 50ml freshly squeezed lime juice
- 1 tablespoon raw honey
- ¼ teaspoon sea salt

INSTRUCTIONS:

Step 1: Grease the air fryer basket with olive oil cooking spray. Add in the salmon and drizzle with fresh lime juice and raw honey; sprinkle with sea salt and pepper.

Step 2: Cook at 180°C for about 10 minutes or until golden brown and cooked through.

Step 3: Divide the salad among serving bowls and top each with the cooked salmon.

Step 4: In a large bowl, mix together the lettuce, rocket, cucumber, tomatoes, red onions, and toasted walnuts. Drizzle with olive oil and balsamic vinegar. Sprinkle with sea salt and pepper. Toss to coat well.

Step 5: Divide the salad among 4 serving bowls and top each with the salmon and avocado. Enjoy!

5. Air Fryer Snapper Fillets With Veggies

The air fryer is the best way to cook red snapper. It's really quick, easy, and the different flavours from the veggies are infused into the fish. The best part is this meal will be ready in only 15 minutes!

PREPARATION TIME: 10 MINUTES
COOKING TIME: 15 MINUTES
PER SERVING (2): KCAL: 319; FAT: 12G; CARBS: 29G; PROTEIN: 19G; SUGARS: 9G; FIBRE: 8G.

INGRENKEDIENTS:

- 2 boneless red snapper fillets
- 120g leeks, chopped
- 120g green bell pepper, chopped
- 120g red bell pepper, chopped
- 1 tablespoon extra virgin olive oil
- 60ml white wine
- 2 teaspoons dried tarragon
- ¼ teaspoon sea salt
- ¼ teaspoon black pepper

INSTRUCTIONS:

Step 1: In a baking dish that fits into your air fryer, toss together the red snapper fillets, leeks, red bell pepper, green bell pepper, tarragon, oil, wine, sea salt, and pepper.

Step 2: Place the dish in the air fryer and cook at 180°C for 15 minutes, flipping the fish halfway.

Step 3: Divide the red snapper fillets and the vegetables among serving plates and serve.

6. Air-Fried Fish and Chips

Fish and chips is a firm favourite in many households! This air-fried fish and chips recipe is a healthier and guilt-free way to enjoy one of your favourite meals. Ready in minutes, the potatoes and fish are crisp on the outside and soft and flaky on the inside.

PREPARATION TIME: 15 MINUTES
COOKING TIME: 30 MINUTES
PER SERVING (4): KCAL: 307; FAT: 9G; CARBS: 31G; PROTEIN: 26G; SUGARS: 2G; FIBRE: 4G.

INGREDIENTS:

- 2 tablespoons extra virgin olive oil
- 3 russet potatoes, peeled and sliced into thin sticks
- 1 tablespoon sea salt
- 1 teaspoon black pepper
- 450g tilapia fillet
- 1 free-range egg
- 60g all-purpose flour
- 250g breadcrumbs

NSTRUCTIONS:

Step 1: In a large bowl, toss together the sliced potatoes, olive oil, sea salt, and pepper.

Step 2: Preheat your air fryer to 200°C.

Step 3: Transfer the coated potatoes into the air fryer basket and cook for about 20 minutes, stirring halfway through.

Step 4: Meanwhile, beat the egg in a small bowl.

Step 5: Add the flour in a separate bowl and the breadcrumbs in another.

Step 6: Dredge the tilapia fillets in the flour, then dip in the egg and lastly the breadcrumbs.

Step 7: Remove the chips from the air fryer; then add the tilapia fillets to the air fryer basket and cook at 165°C for 15 minutes, turning halfway through.

Step 8: Serve the chips and fish with your favourite sauce.

7. Lemon and Cajun Air Fryer Salmon

This lemon and Cajun air fryer salmon is flavourful and spicy with a hint of sweetness. Delicious and soft, serve it with mashed potatoes or air-fried potatoes, and drizzle with your favourite sauce.

PREPARATION TIME: 10 MINUTES
COOKING TIME: 10 MINUTES
PER SERVING (2): KCAL: 327; FAT: 19G; CARBS: 4G; PROTEIN: 34G; SUGARS: 2G; FIBRE: 0.3G.

INGRENKEDIENTS:

* 2 150g salmon fillets, with skin on
* Olive oil cooking spray
* 30ml fresh lemon juice
* 2 teaspoons brown sugar
* 3 teaspoons Cajun seasoning

INSTRUCTIONS:

Step 1: Preheat your air fryer to 180°C.

Step 2: Spray the salmon fillets with olive oil cooking spray.

Step 3: In a small bowl, mix together the fresh lemon juice, Cajun seasoning, sea salt, and brown sugar until well blended; rub over the salmon fillets and place in the air fryer basket.

Step 4: Cook for about 10 minutes or until the fish is cooked through.

8. Simple Air Fryer Catfish

If you're looking for crispy catfish with a beautiful crunch with every bite, then look no further than this simple air fryer catfish. Perfectly seasoned and using very little oil, you will enjoy every bite and save yourself a tonne of calories by using an air fryer instead of deep frying.

PREPARATION TIME: 10 MINUTES
COOKING TIME: 40 MINUTES
PER SERVING (3): KCAL: 423; FAT: 38G; CARBS: 15G; PROTEIN: 30G; SUGARS: 0.1G; FIBRE: 2G.

INGREDIENTS:

* 3 catfish fillets
* 1 tablespoon extra virgin olive oil
* ¼ teaspoon sea salt
* ¼ teaspoon black pepper
* 2 tablespoons parsley, chopped

INSTRUCTIONS:

Step 1: Preheat your air fryer to 200°C.

Step 2: Rinse the catfish under running water, then sprinkle with sea salt and pepper until well coated.

Step 3: Drizzle with olive oil and add to the air fryer basket.

Step 4: Cook for about 10 minutes, then turn over the fillets to cook the other sides for another 10 minutes or until golden brown and crispy.

Step 5: Serve the catfish hot, garnished with fresh parsley.

9. Air-Fried Salmon Fish Cakes

These tasty air-fried salmon fish cakes are reminiscent of the authentic and traditional salmon croquettes, pillow soft and moist on the inside and crisp and crunchy on the outside.

PREPARATION TIME: 1 HOUR
COOKING TIME: 10 MINUTES
PER SERVING (6): KCAL: 398; FAT: 28G; CARBS: 12G; PROTEIN: 21G; SUGARS: 3G; FIBRE: 2G.

INGRENKEDIENTS:

- 2 large salmon fillets, ground
- 2 free-range eggs
- 30ml fresh lemon juice
- 50g chives, minced
- 50g mayonnaise
- 1 carrot, thinly grated
- 1 red onion, minced
- 30g cornmeal
- 20g Italian seasoning
- 1 teaspoon sea salt
- ½ teaspoon black pepper

INSTRUCTIONS:

Step 1: In a large bowl, mix together the salmon, grated carrots, and minced red onion. Add in the eggs, mayonnaise, cornmeal, Italian seasoning, minced chives, sea salt, and fresh lemon juice until well combined.

Step 2: Form small patties from the salmon mixture and place them in a baking pan. Cover with foil and refrigerate for at least 1 hour or until firm.

Step 3: Transfer the salmon patties and place them into the air fryer basket in a single layer.

Step 4: Spray with olive oil and cook in the air fryer at 200°C for about 5 minutes per side or until golden brown.

Step 5: Serve with your favourite dip.

10. Crispy Air Fryer Prawns With Hot and Sweet Sauce

Make crispy air fryer prawns that are soft and juicy in the centre and crisp on the outside. These are perfect for dunking in the hot and sweet sauce.

PREPARATION TIME: 10 MINUTES
COOKING TIME: 8 MINUTES
PER SERVING (4): KCAL: 302; FAT: 25G; CARBS: 14G; PROTEIN: 19G; SUGARS: 3G; FIBRE: 6G.

INGREDIENTS:

For the prawns:

- 500g prawns, peeled, deveined, and cleaned
- 180g panko breadcrumbs
- 120g all-purpose flour
- 1 large free-range egg white
- 1 large free-range egg
- 1 teaspoon chicken seasoning
- 1 teaspoon sweet paprika
- ¼ teaspoon pepper
- ¼ teaspoon sea salt

For the hot and sweet sauce:

- 80ml Greek yoghurt
- 60g sweet chilli sauce
- 30g sriracha
- Olive oil cooking spray

INSTRUCTIONS:

Step 1: Make the sauce by combining all the sauce ingredients in a bowl; set aside.

Step 2: Preheat your air fryer to 200°C.

Step 3: In a small bowl, beat together the egg, egg white, and sea salt until well combined.

Step 4: Add the flour and crumbs in 2 separate small bowls.

Step 5: Season the prawns with chicken seasoning, sea salt, paprika, and black pepper, then dip into the flour, egg mix, and lastly the crumbs.

Step 6: Spray the prawns with olive oil cooking spray and place in the air fryer basket.

Step 7: Cook for 4 minutes, then stir to flip them over.

Step 8: Continue cooking for 4 minutes or until crispy and golden brown.

11. Tasty Air-Fried Cod

In less than 20 minutes, you will have tasty air-fried cod that has the perfect outer crust, a moist and flaky inside, and a delicious tangy flavour.

PREPARATION TIME: 10 MINUTES
COOKING TIME: 12 MINUTES
PER SERVING (4): KCAL: 399; FAT: 17G; CARBS: 24G; PROTEIN: 28G; SUGARS: 13G; FIBRE: 8G.

INGRENKEDIENTS:

- 2 120g cod fillets
- 1 teaspoon sesame oil
- 2 tablespoons fresh lime juice
- ¼ teaspoon sea salt
- ¼ teaspoon black pepper
- 250ml water
- 50ml soy sauce
- 3 teaspoons brown sugar
- 3 tablespoons extra virgin olive oil
- 60g ginger, sliced
- 250g spring onions, chopped
- 30g fresh coriander, chopped

INSTRUCTIONS:

Step 1: In a small bowl, mix together the fresh lime juice, lime zest, sesame oil, sea salt, and pepper; rub and the mixture over the fish and let sit for at least 10 minutes.

Step 2: Place the fish in the air fryer basket and cook at 180°C for 12 minutes.

Step 3: Meanwhile, add the soy sauce, brown sugar, and water to a pan and simmer for about 5 minutes or until the sugar is dissolved. Set aside.

Step 4: Heat the olive oil in a skillet and stir in the green onions and ginger. Sauté for 5 minutes, then remove from the heat.

Step 5: Divide the fish among serving plates and top with the green onion mixture. Drizzle each serving with the soy sauce mixture and sprinkle with chopped coriander. Enjoy!

12. Air-Fried Lemon Catfish

Lemon juice is the star of this air-fried catfish recipe. Blending perfectly with sweet paprika, black pepper, sea salt, olive oil, and fresh parsley, it adds deep flavour to this crispy fried catfish.

PREPARATION TIME: 10 MINUTES
COOKING TIME: 20 MINUTES
PER SERVING (4): KCAL: 253; FAT: 7G; CARBS: 26G; PROTEIN: 23G; SUGARS: 3G; FIBRE: 6G.

INGREDIENTS:

- 4 catfish fillets
- 1 tablespoon extra virgin olive oil
- 20ml fresh lemon juice
- ¼ teaspoon sweet paprika
- ¼ teaspoon sea salt
- ¼ teaspoon black pepper
- 20g parsley, chopped

INSTRUCTIONS:

Step 1: In a small bowl, mix half of the fresh lemon juice, olive oil, paprika, sea salt, and pepper until well combined. Rub the mixture over the catfish fillets and place in the air fryer basket.

Step 2: Cook for 200°C for 20 minutes, flipping them halfway.

Step 3: Divide among serving plates and drizzle each with the remaining fresh lemon juice, and top with chopped parsley.

13. Cod Fillets With Pecans

This air fryer cod fillets with pecans recipe will change how you cook fish forever! You will enjoy this golden and crispy outside, the flaky and moist inside, and the crunchy pecan mix that balances the cod perfectly!

PREPARATION TIME: 10 MINUTES
COOKING TIME: 15 MINUTES
PER SERVING (2): KCAL: 322; FAT: 9G; CARBS: 32G; PROTEIN: 21G; SUGARS: 19G; FIBRE: 11G.

INGRENKEDIENTS:

*   2 black cod fillets, boneless
*   1 tablespoon extra virgin olive oil
*   250g pecans
*   250g grapes, halved
*   1 fennel bulb, sliced
*   ¼ teaspoon sea salt
*   ¼ teaspoon black pepper

INSTRUCTIONS:

Step 1: Drizzle half of the olive oil over the fish and sprinkle with sea salt and pepper; rub well and place the fish in the air fryer basket.

Step 2: Cook at 200°C for 10 minutes.

Step 3: In a large bowl, mix the pecans, grapes, the remaining oil, fennel, sea salt, and pepper; toss to coat well, then transfer to a pan that fits into your air fryer. Cook for 5 minutes at 200°C.

Step 4: Divide the fish among the serving plates and top with the pecan mix.

14. Air Fryer Lemon Salmon

This sweet and sour air fryer lemon salmon is easy and quick, and it packs a tonne of flavour. Serve with steamed veggies or air-fried potatoes.

PREPARATION TIME: 1 HOUR
COOKING TIME: 15 MINUTES
PER SERVING (2): KCAL: 399; FAT: 2G; CARBS: 28G; PROTEIN: 24G; SUGARS: 21G; FIBRE: 3G.

INGREDIENTS:

*   2 salmon fillets
*   4 tablespoons raw honey
*   50ml fresh lemon juice
*   60ml soy sauce
*   1 teaspoon water
*   ¼ teaspoon sea salt
*   ¼ teaspoon black pepper

NSTRUCTIONS:

Step 1: In a large bowl, mix the raw honey, soy sauce, lemon juice, lemon zest, water, sea salt, and pepper until well combined.

Step 2: Add in the salmon fillets and toss to coat well; marinate for at least 1 hour in the fridge.

Step 3: Transfer the salmon to the air fryer basket and cook for 15 minutes at 180°C, flipping halfway.

Step 4: Meanwhile, add the marinade to a skillet and cook over medium heat for 5 minutes or until thickened.

Step 5: Divide the salmon fillets among serving plates and drizzle with the sauce.

15. Spiced Cod in Lime and Plum Sauce

Spiced to perfection and cooked in the air fryer, this cod recipe is absolutely delicious and so easy to make. The plum sauce adds elegance to the dish, making it perfect for a special night.

PREPARATION TIME: 10 MINUTES
COOKING TIME: 20 MINUTES
PER SERVING (2): KCAL: 311; FAT: 7G; CARBS: 17G; PROTEIN: 19G; SUGARS: 6G; FIBRE: 2G.

INGRENKEDIENTS:

- 2 large cod fillets
- 1 tablespoon extra virgin olive oil
- 120ml plum sauce
- 60ml fresh lime juice
- ¼ teaspoon turmeric powder
- ½ teaspoon ginger powder
- ½ teaspoon garlic powder
- ¼ teaspoon sea salt
- ¼ teaspoon black pepper

INSTRUCTIONS:

Step 1: In a small bowl, mix together the oil, half of the fresh lime juice, spices, sea salt, and pepper until well combined.

Step 2: Rub the lime-spice mix over the cod fillets and place into the air fryer basket.

Step 3: Cook in the air fryer at 180°C for 15 minutes, flipping halfway.

Step 4: Meanwhile, add the plum sauce and the remaining lime juice into a skillet and cook for 2 minutes.

Step 5: Divide the cod between 2 serving plates and drizzle each with plum sauce. Enjoy!

16. Simple Air-Fried Salmon With Fresh Scallions

Skip the oven for this one and make this simple air-fried salmon with fresh scallions for an easy, flavourful weeknight dinner that's ready in only 10 minutes!

PREPARATION TIME: 1 HOUR
COOKING TIME: 8 MINUTES
PER SERVING (2): KCAL: 412; FAT: 12G; CARBS: 29G; PROTEIN: 23G; SUGARS: 17G; FIBRE: 10G.

INGREDIENTS:

- 2 salmon fillets
- 30ml fresh lemon juice
- 30ml extra virgin olive oil
- 80g brown sugar
- 80ml soy sauce
- 80ml water
- ½ teaspoon garlic powder
- ¼ teaspoon sea salt
- ¼ teaspoon black pepper
- 120g fresh scallions, chopped

NSTRUCTIONS:

Step 1: In a large bowl, mix the fresh lemon juice, brown sugar, garlic powder, soy sauce, oil, water, sea salt, and pepper until well combined; add in the salmon fillets and toss to coat well.

Step 2: Let the fish marinate for at least 1 hour in the fridge.

Step 3: Transfer the salmon fillets to the air fryer basket and cook for 10 minutes at 180°C, flipping halfway.

Step 4: Divide the fish among serving plates topped with chopped scallions. Enjoy!

17. Lemon and Chilli Tilapia

This air fryer lemon and chilli tilapia is a light, flaky, delicious, and flavourful meal that only takes 10 minutes to make; perfect for a busy weeknight.

PREPARATION TIME: 10 MINUTES
COOKING TIME: 10 MINUTES
PER SERVING (4): KCAL: 322; FAT: 4G; CARBS: 12G; PROTEIN: 25G; SUGARS: 4G; FIBRE: 7G.

INGRENKEDIENTS:

- 4 tilapia fillets
- 60ml fresh lemon juice
- 4 cloves garlic, minced
- 30ml extra virgin olive oil
- 1 teaspoon chilli powder
- ¼ teaspoon sea salt
- ¼ teaspoon black pepper

INSTRUCTIONS:

Step 1: In a small bowl, mix the fresh lemon juice, chilli powder, olive oil, minced garlic, sea salt, and pepper until well combined.

Step 2: Rub the lemon-chilli mix over the tilapia fillets and place in the air fryer basket.

Step 3: Cook at 180°C for 10 minutes, flipping the fish halfway.

Step 4: Divide the fish among serving plates and serve right away.

18. Cod in Lemony Tomato Sauce

This cod in lemony tomato sauce is an easy, quick, and light cod recipe. It's cooked in the air fryer and infused with lemon flavour, then served with a delicious tomato sauce. Healthy and low carb, it can be enjoyed with a side of veggies.

PREPARATION TIME: 10 MINUTES
COOKING TIME: 15 MINUTES
PER SERVING (4): KCAL: 300; FAT: 5G; CARBS: 22G; PROTEIN: 8G; SUGARS: 10G; FIBRE: 8G.

INGREDIENTS:

- 2 tablespoons extra virgin olive oil
- 4 skinless and boneless cod fillets
- 250g red onions, chopped
- 12 cherry tomatoes, halved
- 8 black olives, chopped
- 30ml fresh lemon juice
- 60g basil, chopped
- ¼ teaspoon sea salt
- ¼ teaspoon black pepper

NSTRUCTIONS:

Step 1: Season the fish with sea salt and pepper, and place in the air fryer basket.

Step 2: Cook at 180°C for 10 minutes, flipping halfway.

Step 3: Heat the olive oil in a skillet over medium heat and sauté the red onions for 5 minutes.

Step 4: Stir in the tomatoes and olives and cook for about 5 minutes or until the tomatoes are softened. Stir in the fresh lemon juice, chopped basil, sea salt, and pepper, and cook for another 5 minutes.

Step 5: Divide the fish among serving plates and drizzle with the tomato sauce.

19. Crab and Prawn Casserole

This air fryer crab and prawn casserole is the perfect weeknight dish that's super tasty and quick to make. Ready in only 25 minutes, you will enjoy the combination of flavours and how easy it is to prepare this dish.

PREPARATION TIME: 10 MINUTES
COOKING TIME: 25 MINUTES
PER SERVING (4): KCAL: 221; FAT: 13G; CARBS: 17G; PROTEIN: 19G; SUGARS: 7G; FIBRE: 9G.

INGRENKEDIENTS:

- 250g flaked crabmeat
- 500g prawns, peeled and deveined
- 120g yellow onion, chopped
- 250g celery, chopped
- 250g green bell pepper, chopped
- 250g mayonnaise
- 1 teaspoon Worcestershire sauce
- 1 teaspoon sweet paprika
- 30g breadcrumbs
- 20g butter, melted
- ¼ teaspoon sea salt
- ¼ teaspoon black pepper

INSTRUCTIONS:

Step 1: In a large bowl, mix together the crabmeat, prawns, onion, bell pepper, celery, mayonnaise, Worcestershire sauce, sea salt, and pepper.

Step 2: Transfer to a baking dish that fits into your air fryer. Sprinkle with paprika and breadcrumbs, and drizzle with melted butter.

Step 3: Cook in the air fryer at 160°C for 25 minutes, stirring halfway.

Step 4: Divide the casserole among serving plates and serve immediately.

20. Air Fryer Seafood Casserole

There is nothing better than an air-fried seafood casserole with crispy breadcrumbs and cheese on top and the moist, juicy, creamy, flavourful meat inside. This is the ultimate comfort food!

PREPARATION TIME: 10 MINUTES
COOKING TIME: 40 MINUTES
PER SERVING (6): KCAL: 370; FAT: 32G; CARBS: 28G; PROTEIN: 23G; SUGARS: 11G; FIBRE: 16G.

INGREDIENTS:

- 90g butter
- 1 yellow onion, chopped
- 250g lobster meat, diced
- 250g skinless, boneless haddock, diced
- 4 scallops, sliced
- 250g mushrooms, chopped
- 120g green bell pepper, chopped
- 120g celery, chopped
- 120ml white wine
- 1 tablespoon fresh lemon juice
- 2 garlic cloves, minced
- 120ml heavy cream
- 400ml milk
- 120g flour
- ½ teaspoon mustard powder
- 50g cheddar cheese, grated
- 80g breadcrumbs
- 120g parsley, chopped
- 1 teaspoon sweet paprika
- 1 teaspoon each of sea salt and black pepper

INSTRUCTIONS:

Step 1: Heat 4 tablespoons of butter in a skillet over medium heat and sauté the onions, garlic, celery, mushrooms, and bell peppers for 5 minutes. Stir in the wine and cook for 5 minutes.

Step 2: Stir in the milk, cream, flour, and cook for 6 minutes.

Step 3: Stir in the fresh lemon juice, haddock, scallops, lobster, mustard, sea salt, and pepper. Transfer the seafood mix to a baking dish that fits into your air fryer.

Step 4: In a small bowl, whisk together the remaining butter, cheese, paprika, and breadcrumbs; sprinkle over the seafood.

Step 5: Cook in the air fryer at 180°C for 16 minutes.

Step 6: Divide the casserole among serving plates and serve topped with chopped parsley.

21. Air-Fried Trout in Green Onion-Orange Sauce

A delicious, quick, and easy version of the classic fish filet l'orange, this trout is air fried to perfection with a crisp top and a moist and flaky inside in a deliciously flavoured orange sauce.

PREPARATION TIME: 10 MINUTES
COOKING TIME: 10 MINUTES
PER SERVING (4): KCAL: 239; FAT: 10G; CARBS: 18G; PROTEIN: 23G; SUGARS: 10G; FIBRE: 7G.

INGRENKEDIENTS:

*   4 trout fillets, skinless and boneless
*   250g green onions, chopped
*   1 tablespoon extra virgin olive oil
*   2 tablespoons brown sugar
*   30g ginger, grated
*   5 garlic cloves
*   60ml fresh orange juice
*   30g orange zest
*   ¼ teaspoon sea salt
*   ¼ teaspoon black pepper

INSTRUCTIONS:

Step 1: In a food processor, process together garlic, fresh ginger, olive oil, brown sugar, fresh orange juice, orange zest, sea salt, and pepper until smooth.

Step 2: Add to a baking dish that fits into your air fryer and toss in trout fillets until well coated with the mixture.

Step 3: Sprinkle the fish with chopped green onions and cook at 180°C for 10 minutes.

Step 4: Divide the fish among serving plates and drizzle each serving with the sauce. Enjoy!

22. Air Fryer Salmon in Blackberry Sauce

This beautiful air fryer salmon in blackberry sauce is a light, moist, and flaky fish recipe that packs a tonne of flavour and is ready in about half an hour. Serve with a side of fresh salad, steamed veggies with rice, mashed potatoes, or air-fried potatoes.

PREPARATION TIME: 10 MINUTES
COOKING TIME: 33 MINUTES
PER SERVING (4): KCAL: 312; FAT: 4G; CARBS: 19G; PROTEIN: 14G; SUGARS: 11G; FIBRE: 9G.

INGREDIENTS:

*   4 medium salmon fillets
*   1 tablespoon extra virgin olive oil
*   400g blackberries
*   30ml fresh lemon juice
*   20g fresh ginger, grated
*   250ml water
*   60g brown sugar
*   ¼ teaspoon sea salt
*   ¼ teaspoon black pepper

INSTRUCTIONS:

Step 1: In a pan, add water, lemon juice, blackberries, and ginger; bring to a rolling boil. Then simmer for 5 minutes.

Step 2: Remove from the heat, strain into a bowl, then return to the pan. Stir in the brown sugar until it dissolves and simmer over medium heat for 20 minutes or until the sauce is thick.

Step 3: Let the sauce to cool, then brush it over the salmon. Sprinkle with sea salt and pepper, then drizzle with olive oil.

Step 4: Place the fish into the air fryer basket and cook at 180°C for 10 minutes, flipping the fish once.

Step 5: Divide the fish among serving plates and serve drizzled with the remaining blackberry sauce.

23. Delicious French Cod

This easy one-pot cod dish is an air fryer take on the classic cod Provençal recipe. With a delicious combination of butter, tomato, wine, parsley, garlic, and olive oil and a soft, flaky and juicy cod, you are going to enjoy this quick, healthy, and super-tasty dish.

PREPARATION TIME: 10 MINUTES
COOKING TIME: 22 MINUTES
PER SERVING (4): KCAL: 261; FAT: 8G; CARBS: 26G; PROTEIN: 14G; SUGARS: 9G; FIBRE: 12G.

INGRENKEDIENTS:

- 1kg cod, boneless
- 30ml olive oil
- 30g butter
- 1 yellow onion, chopped
- 120ml white wine
- 2 garlic cloves, minced
- 300g canned tomatoes
- 40g parsley, chopped
- ¼ teaspoon sea salt
- ¼ teaspoon black pepper

INSTRUCTIONS:

Step 1: Heat olive oil in a skillet over medium heat, and sauté the yellow onion and garlic for 5 minutes or until fragrant.

Step 2: Stir in the wine for 1 minute, then add in the tomatoes. Cook for 2 minutes or until the tomatoes are soft.

Step 3: Remove from the heat and stir in the chopped parsley. Pour the mixture into a baking dish that fits into your air fryer.

Step 4: Add in the fish and cook at 180°C for 15 minutes.

Step 5: Divide among serving plates and serve right away!

24. Special Catfish Fillets

These catfish fillets are marinated in a zingy and buttery sauce that has dense flavours, which are then air fried to crisp and flaky perfection. Enjoy!

PREPARATION TIME: 10 MINUTES
COOKING TIME: 12 MINUTES
PER SERVING (4): KCAL: 351; FAT: 8G; CARBS: 27G; PROTEIN: 17G; SUGARS: 4G; FIBRE: 16G.

INGREDIENTS:

- 2 catfish fillets
- 30g butter
- ½ teaspoon garlic, minced
- 180g ketchup
- 20ml balsamic vinegar
- 60g Worcestershire sauce
- 1 teaspoon mustard
- ½ teaspoon jerk seasoning
- 20g parsley, chopped
- ¼ teaspoon sea salt
- ¼ teaspoon black pepper

INSTRUCTIONS:

Step 1: Heat the butter in a skillet over medium heat; stir in the garlic, ketchup, Worcestershire sauce, vinegar, mustard, jerk seasoning, sea salt, and pepper. Cook for about 5 minutes, then remove from the heat.

Step 2: Add the catfish fillets and stir until the fish is well coated with the sauce.

Step 3: Let the fish marinate for at least 10 minutes, then drain.

Step 4: Place the fillets into the air fryer basket and cook at 180°C for 10 minutes, flipping the fish halfway.

Step 5: Divide the catfish fillets among serving plates and serve right away!

25. Air Fryer Tilapia in Coconut Sauce

Unbelievably moist and flaky, this air fryer tilapia in coconut sauce is sure going to be one of your go-to fish dishes. The coconut milk, jalapeno, garlic, ginger, garam masala, and coriander infuse intense flavour into the tilapia, and it only takes 30 minutes from start to finish!

PREPARATION TIME: 10 MINUTES
COOKING TIME: 20 MINUTES
PER SERVING (4): KCAL: 200; FAT: 5G; CARBS: 25G; PROTEIN: 26G; SUGARS: 7G; FIBRE: 6G.

iNGRENKEDIENTS:

- 120ml coconut milk
- 2 garlic cloves, chopped
- 1 teaspoon ginger, grated
- ½ jalapeno, chopped
- ½ teaspoon garam masala
- 120g coriander, chopped
- ¼ teaspoon sea salt
- ¼ teaspoon black pepper
- 1 tablespoon olive oil
- 4 medium tilapia fillets

iNSTRUCTiONS:

Step 1: Add the coconut milk, garlic, ginger, jalapeno, coriander, garam masala, sea salt, and pepper into a food processor. Process until very smooth.

Step 2: Heat olive oil in a skillet and sear the tilapia fillets for 5 minutes per side or until golden brown.

Step 3: Transfer to a baking dish that fits into your air fryer and pour over the coconut milk mixture.

Step 4: Place the dish into the air fryer and cook at 200°C for 10 minutes.

Step 5: Divide the fish among serving plates and serve.

26. Air Fryer Tilapia in Lemon-Chive Sauce

This air fryer tilapia is simple, quick, easy and extremely delicious with a crisp exterior and moist and flaky interior. Served with Greek yoghurt, lemon, and chive sauce, this recipe is nothing short of amazing. Add some air-fried chips for an out-of-this-world dinner!

PREPARATION TIME: 10 MINUTES
COOKING TIME: 8 MINUTES
PER SERVING (4): KCAL: 261; FAT: 8G; CARBS: 24G; PROTEIN: 21G; SUGARS: 5G; FIBRE: 18G.

iNGREDIENTS:

- 4 medium tilapia fillets
- 1 tablespoon olive oil
- 60ml Greek yoghurt
- 1 tablespoon raw honey
- 30g chives, chopped
- 30ml fresh lemon juice
- ¼ teaspoon sea salt
- ¼ teaspoon black pepper

NSTRUCTiONS:

Step 1: Drizzle the tilapia fillets with olive oil and sprinkle with sea salt and pepper; rub well and place into your air fryer basket.

Step 2: Cook at 180°C for 10 minutes, flipping the fish halfway.

Step 3: In a large bowl, mix together the Greek yoghurt, fresh lemon juice, raw honey, chives, sea salt, and pepper until well combined.

Step 4: Divide the fish onto serving plates and drizzle each with the yoghurt sauce. Enjoy!

27. Air-Fried Orange-Honey Sea Bass With Lentils

This air fryer orange-honey sea bass with lentils is one of the tastiest, healthiest fish dishes you can make. Ready in less than 30 minutes, from start to finish, all that's left is to serve this dish with a side of fresh salad or steamed veggies.

PREPARATION TIME: 10 MINUTES
COOKING TIME: 10 MINUTES
PER SERVING (2): KCAL: 212; FAT: 8G; CARBS: 12G; PROTEIN: 17G; SUGARS: 2G; FIBRE: 9G.

INGRENKEDIENTS:

- 2 sea bass fillets
- 2 tablespoons extra virgin olive oil
- 20g fresh orange zest
- 30ml fresh orange juice
- 30g mustard
- 1 tablespoon raw honey
- 250g canned lentils
- 60g watercress
- 60g dill, chopped
- 60g parsley, chopped
- ¼ teaspoon sea salt
- ¼ teaspoon black pepper

INSTRUCTIONS:

Step 1: In a small bowl, mix together the fresh orange juice, zest, raw honey, olive oil, mustard, sea salt, and pepper; rub over the fish and place it in the air fryer basket.

Step 2: Cook the fish at 180°C for 10 minutes, flipping the fish halfway.

Step 3: Add the lentils to a skillet and stir in the dill, watercress, parsley, and the remaining oil.

Step 4: Cook for 5 minutes or until warmed through.

Step 5: Serve the fish with the lentil mixture on the side.

28. Air Fryer Cod With Red Onions

This air fryer cod with red onions is one of the best ways of cooking moist and flaky cod with delicious veggies all in one pot. It's quick and easy, and the veggies are deliciously caramelised to complement the crispy fish. Absolutely amazing!

PREPARATION TIME: 10 MINUTES
COOKING TIME: 15 MINUTES
PER SERVING (2): KCAL: 270; FAT: 14G; CARBS: 14G; PROTEIN: 22G; SUGARS: 0.1G; FIBRE: 8G.

INGREDIENTS:

- 2 medium cod fillets
- 2 tablespoons extra virgin olive oil
- 500g red onions, sliced
- 250g mushrooms, sliced
- 2 teaspoons dried thyme
- 3 teaspoons dried parsley
- ¼ teaspoon sea salt
- ¼ teaspoon black pepper

INSTRUCTIONS:

Step 1: Place the cod fillets in a baking dish that fits into your air fryer.

Step 2: Add the sliced red onions, mushrooms, olive oil, thyme, parsley, sea salt, and pepper.

Step 3: Toss to combine well, then cook in the air fryer at 200°C for 15 minutes.

Step 4: Divide the meal among serving plates and serve.

SNACKS AND APPETISERS

Don't Forget To Get The Color Images FREE!
Simply Scan The QR Code Below!

Hello! Please scan the QR code below to access your promised bonus of all our recipes with full colored photos & beautiful designs! It is the best we could do to keep the book as cheap as possible while providing the best value!

Also, once downloaded you can take the PDF with you digitally wherever you go- meaning you can cook these recipes wherever an Air Fryer is present!

STEP BY STEP Guide-

1. *Open Your Phones (Or Any Device You Want The Book On) Back Camera. The Back Camera Is The One You use as if you are taking a picture of someone.*

2. *Simply point your Camera at the QR code and 'tap' the QR code with your finger to focus the camera.*

3. *A link / pop up will appear. Simply tap that (and make sure you have internet connection) and the FREE PDF containing all of the colored images should appear.*

4. *If You Click On The File And It Says 'The File Is Too Big To Preview' Simply click 'Download' and it will download the full book onto your phone!*

5. *Now you have access to these FOREVER. Simply 'Bookmark' The tab it opened on, or download the document and take wherever you want.*

6. *Repeat this on any device you want it on!*

Any Issues / Feedback / Troubleshooting please email:
anthonypublishing123@gmail.com *and our customer service team will help you! We want to make sure you have the BEST experience with our books!*

1. Cheesy Bacon-Stuffed Mushrooms

These cheesy bacon-stuffed mushrooms are savoury, creamy, crunchy, and juicy. The veggies add a welcome sweetness and texture.

PREPARATION TIME: 20 MINUTES
COOKING TIME: 20 MINUTES
PER SERVING (12): KCAL: 43; FAT: 3G; CARBS: 2G; PROTEIN: 2G; SUGARS: 0.5G; FIBRE: 1.2G.

INGRENKEDIENTS:

- 24 mushrooms, stems and caps (diced)
- 2 slices bacon, diced
- 1 red onion, diced
- 1 red bell pepper, diced
- 1 carrot, diced
- 250g cheddar cheese, grated
- 120ml sour cream
- 30g cheddar cheese, grated

INSTRUCTIONS:

Step 1: Preheat your air fryer to 180°C.

Step 2: Cook bacon in a skillet set over medium heat for about 5 minutes or until crispy and golden brown.

Step 3: Transfer to a plate and set aside.

Step 4: Add the onion, carrots, mushroom stems, and bell pepper to the bacon grease, and cook for 5 minutes or until the vegetables are tender.

Step 5: Stir in the cheddar cheese and sour cream, and cook for 2 minutes or until the cheese is melted.

Step 6: Preheat your air fryer to 180°C.

Step 7: Stuff the mushroom caps with the bacon mixture and sprinkle with extra cheddar cheese on top.

Step 8: Place the stuffed mushroom in the air fryer basket and cook for about 10 minutes or until the cheese is melted.

Step 9: Remove the mushrooms from the air fryer and serve right away!

2. Air Fryer Courgette Chips

These air fryer courgette chips are a great low-carb snack that are crisp on the outside with a juicy and flavourful inside.

PREPARATION TIME: 15 MINUTES
COOKING TIME: 20 MINUTES
PER SERVING (3): KCAL: 173; FAT: 6G; CARBS: 21G; PROTEIN: 10G; SUGARS: 5G; FIBRE: 4G.

INGREDIENTS:

- 3 courgettes, sliced into sticks
- 120g breadcrumbs
- 30g Parmesan cheese, grated
- ¼ teaspoon garlic powder
- 2 free-range eggs
- ¼ teaspoon sea salt
- ¼ teaspoon black pepper

INSTRUCTIONS:

Step 1: Preheat your air fryer to 200°C.

Step 2: In a small bowl, whisk together the eggs, sea salt, and pepper until well combined.

Step 3: In another bowl, mix the cheese, breadcrumbs, and garlic powder until well combined.

Step 4: Dip the sliced courgette in the egg mixture and coat with the crumb mixture.

Step 5: Place them in the air fryer basket and cook for about 10 minutes; flip the courgette sticks over and continue cooking for another 10 minutes or until the courgette chips are cooked through and crispy.

Step 6: Serve with your favourite sauce.

3. Air-Fried Sweet Potato Chips

These simple and quick air fryer sweet potato chips are crisp and crunchy on the outside and pillow soft on the inside. You can enjoy them as is with a ketchup dip or serve them alongside your favourite mains.

PREPARATION TIME: 10 MINUTES
COOKING TIME: 20 MINUTES
PER SERVING (4): KCAL: 97; FAT: 2G; CARBS: 20G; PROTEIN: 3G; SUGARS: 2G; FIBRE: 0.3G.

INGRENKEDIENTS:

* 500g sweet potatoes, sliced into half-inch sticks
* 1 teaspoon extra virgin olive oil
* ¼ teaspoon sea salt

INSTRUCTIONS:

Step 1: Preheat your air fryer to 200°C.

Step 2: Peel the sweet potatoes and slice into half-inch sticks.

Step 3: Add to a large bowl and stir in the olive oil until well coated.

Step 4: Transfer to the air fryer basket and cook for 20 minutes, tossing every 5 minutes.

Step 5: Remove from the air fryer and sprinkle with sea salt.

Step 6: Serve warm.

4. Air-Fried Chickpeas

These air-fried chickpeas are the crispiest, crunchiest, most flavourful, and healthiest snack you will find. Perfect for a movie night or any time you need a quick pick-me-up.

PREPARATION TIME: 5 MINUTES
COOKING TIME: 15 MINUTES
PER SERVING (4): KCAL: 241; FAT: 6G; CARBS: 36G; PROTEIN: 11G; SUGARS: 6G; FIBRE: 10G.

INGREDIENTS:

* 600g canned chickpeas
* 1 tablespoon olive oil
* ⅛ teaspoon salt
* ¼ teaspoon garlic powder
* ¼ teaspoon onion powder
* ½ teaspoon paprika
* ¼ teaspoon cayenne pepper

INSTRUCTIONS:

Step 1: Preheat your air fryer to 200°C.

Step 2: Drain the chickpeas and rinse under running water.

Step 3: Transfer to a large bowl and toss in the remaining ingredients until well coated.

Step 4: Add the chickpea mixture into the air fryer basket.

Step 5: Cook for about 15 minutes, shaking a few times, or until the chickpeas are cooked to your liking.

Step 6: Serve and store the rest in an open container.

5. Air Fryer Cinnamon Biscuit Treats

These air fryer cinnamon biscuit treats are simple to make, and they have a beautiful sweet taste with a fluffy interior and a crisp exterior. The icing sugar adds to the decadence of these treats. Enjoy!

PREPARATION TIME: 35 MINUTES
COOKING TIME: 8 MINUTES
PER SERVING (4): KCAL: 322; FAT: 18G; CARBS: 36.6G; PROTEIN: 4.1G; SUGARS: 11.5G; FIBRE: 1G.

INGRENKEDIENTS:

*   120g cold unsalted butter, diced
*   250g all-purpose flour
*   1 tablespoon baking powder
*   ½ teaspoon sea salt
*   180ml milk
*   4 tablespoons unsalted butter, melted
*   60g brown sugar
*   1 teaspoon ground cinnamon
*   30g icing sugar for serving, optional

INSTRUCTIONS:

Step 1: Preheat your air fryer to 190°C.

Step 2: In a large bowl, sift the flour, salt, and baking powder.

Step 3: Add the diced butter to the flour mixture, and use a fork or your hands to cut the butter to the flour until it resembles coarse crumbs.

Step 4: Mix the milk into the flour mixture while stirring gently using a fork until you get a soft dough, then place the dough on a floured surface.

Step 5: Roll out the dough into a rectangle about a quarter-inch thick. Brush the surface with the melted butter and combine the brown sugar with the cinnamon.

Step 6: Sprinkle the sugar-cinnamon mix on top of the dough surface that you have already brushed with melted butter, then divide the dough into 16 smaller rectangles.

Step 7: Grasp the 2 ends of each strip and twist, then place in the basket of your air fryer. You may have to cook in several batches, depending on the size of your air fryer.

Step 8: Cook for 8 minutes, flipping halfway through the cooking time, until golden and crisp on the outside.

Step 9: Serve hot. You can sprinkle with icing sugar, if desired.

6. Crispy Potato Wedges With Pesto

These crispy potato wedges with pesto are so flavourful and so easy to make. With a deep infusion of flavour from the pesto, a crispy surface, and a soft inside, you will enjoy munching on this delicious snack.

PREPARATION TIME: 10 MINUTES
COOKING TIME: 15 MINUTES
PER SERVING (4): KCAL: 277; FAT: 13.2G; CARBS: 34.5G; PROTEIN: 3.6G; SUGARS: 2.5G; FIBRE: 5.1G.

INGREDIENTS:

*   4 russet potatoes, cut into wedges
*   ¼ teaspoon freshly ground black pepper
*   120ml pesto, homemade or store bought
*   Non-stick olive oil cooking spray

INSTRUCTIONS:

Step 1: Preheat your air fryer to 205°C.

Step 2: Combine the wedge potatoes with 60ml of the pesto and freshly ground black pepper, ensuring the potatoes are evenly coated.

Step 3: Spray the basket of your air fryer with the non-stick olive oil cooking spray and arrange the potatoes in one layer.

Step 4: Cook for 15 minutes, shaking the air fryer basket halfway through cooking or until the potatoes turn brown and are cooked through. Serve hot with the remaining half of the pesto.

7. Bacon-Wrapped Dates

Fruity, nutty, cheesy, and meaty, these air fryer bacon-wrapped dates are the perfect snack. Every bite gives an explosion of beautiful flavours.

PREPARATION TIME: 15 MINUTES
COOKING TIME: 12 MINUTES
PER SERVING (3): KCAL: 399; FAT: 24.2G; CARBS: 38.1G; PROTEIN: 12.5G; SUGARS: 30.8G; FIBRE: 5.3G.

INGRENKEDIENTS:

- 12 large pitted Medjool dates
- 12 pecans
- 50g cheddar cheese, cut into 12 small pieces
- 4 slices bacon, cut into strips
- 12 wooden cocktail sticks

INSTRUCTIONS:

Step 1: Preheat your air fryer to 190°C.

Step 2: Gently open up the dates and fill each cavity (where the pit was removed) with a pecan and a piece of cheese.

Step 3: Wrap each stuffed date with a strip of bacon until fully covered, and use a cocktail stick to secure it.

Step 4: Place the dates in the air fryer basket, and cook for 12 minutes until the bacon is crisp and browned.

Step 5: Take out the cocktail sticks and serve hot.

8. Soft and Buttery Garlic Rolls

Drenched in butter, garlic, parsley, and Parmesan cheese, these soft garlic rolls are the real deal! Enjoy them hot or warm for an explosion of flavour and pillow-soft texture in your mouth.

PREPARATION TIME: 10 MINUTES
COOKING TIME: 12 MINUTES
PER SERVING (6): KCAL: 702; FAT: 54.9G; CARBS: 42G; PROTEIN: 10.1G; SUGARS: 0.2G; FIBRE: 3.4G.

INGREDIENTS:

- 450g pizza dough
- 120g melted unsalted butter, divided
- 2 teaspoons garlic, minced
- 2 teaspoons fresh parsley, chopped
- 2 teaspoons Parmesan cheese

INSTRUCTIONS:

Step 1: Preheat your air fryer to 190°C and prepare a metal baking pan by spraying it with non-stick cooking spray.

Step 2: Divide and roll up the pizza dough into 8 balls and place in the oiled pan.

Step 3: Cover with a clean towel and let it rise for half an hour, then brush the tops with half the melted butter.

Step 4: Bake for 15 minutes, remove from the air fryer and brush with the remaining butter and top with the cheese, garlic, and parsley. Bake for 5 minutes longer.

Step 5: Serve warm.

9. Crispy Crab Wontons

This air fryer crispy crab wontons recipe is super simple, with only 4 ingredients. It delivers a tonne of cheesy flavour. Crunchy and deliciously creamy and cheesy, your taste buds are in for a real treat!

PREPARATION TIME: 20 MINUTES
COOKING TIME: 10 MINUTES
PER SERVING (12): KCAL: 358; FAT: 8.3G; CARBS: 56.4G; PROTEIN: 12.6G; SUGARS: 0.1G; FIBRE: 1.8G.

INGRENKEDIENTS:

- 225g softened cream cheese
- 1 spring onion, finely chopped
- 170g crabmeat
- 1 pack wonton wrappers
- Cooking spray

INSTRUCTIONS:

Step 1: Preheat your air fryer to 205°C.

Step 2: In a large mixing bowl, combine the crabmeat, spring onion, and cream cheese, then set aside.

Step 3: Open the package of wonton wrappers and use water to lightly dampen the outer edges of each wonton wrapper; this will help with sealing the pockets.

Step 4: Place 1 heaped tablespoon of the crab mixture at the centre of each wrapper. Carefully fold the wrapper in half to form a triangle, then press the dampened edges together. Repeat for the remaining crab filling and wrappers.

Step 5: Spray both sides of the triangles with cooking spray, then arrange in the basket of your air fryer in a single layer. You may have to cook in batches, depending on the size of your air fryer.

Step 6: Cook for about 10 minutes until crispy and golden. Serve hot with your favourite dip.

10. Air Fryer Crunchy Onion Rings

These onion rings are delicious, easy to make, and low in calories! Crunchy on the outside, soft on the inside, and beautifully seasoned, you will definitely enjoy munching on them.

PREPARATION TIME: 25 MINUTES
COOKING TIME: 10 MINUTE
PER SERVING (4): KCAL: 190; FAT: 2.3G; CARBS: 36.1G; PROTEIN: 7.1G; SUGARS: 5.3G; FIBRE: 4.1G.

INGREDIENTS:

- 65g all-purpose flour
- 85g panko breadcrumbs
- 2 large yellow onions, cut into half-inch thick slices
- 2 teaspoons chipotle seasoning
- ½ teaspoon freshly ground black pepper
- 120ml buttermilk
- 1 large egg
- Non-stick cooking spray

INSTRUCTIONS:

Step 1: Preheat your air fryer to 205°C.

Step 2: Separate the onion slices into rings, then set aside.

Step 3: In a shallow bowl, combine the flour with the chipotle seasoning. In a separate bowl, lightly beat the egg and the buttermilk, and in another shallow bowl combine the panko breadcrumbs with the freshly ground black pepper.

Step 4: Dip the onion rings in the flour, shaking off any excess, then proceed to add the egg mix and finally the panko bowl.

Step 5: Spray your air fryer basket with cooking spray. Arrange the onion rings in a single layer, then lightly spray with cooking spray. You may have to cook in batches, depending on the size of your air fryer.

Step 6: Cook for about 10 minutes or until golden. Serve hot with your favourite dipping sauce.

11. Sweet and Sour Sticky Wings

These sweet and sticky wings are so juicy and flavourful. The best part about this recipe is the 2-step process of making sticky wings – deep frying the wings and cooking the sauce before tossing in the wings. Quick, easy, and absolutely delicious, this is definitely going to be your go-to sticky wings recipe.

PREPARATION TIME: 20 MINUTES
COOKING TIME: 25 MINUTES
PER SERVING (4): KCAL: 314; FAT: 12.8G; CARBS: 6G; PROTEIN: 44.5G; SUGARS: 0.1G; FIBRE: 0.2G.

INGRENKEDIENTS:

- 900g chicken wing drumettes
- 2 teaspoons Thai red curry paste
- 60ml sweet and sour sauce
- 1 teaspoon light soy sauce
- 2 cloves garlic, minced
- 1 spring onion, thinly sliced
- Non-stick cooking spray

INSTRUCTIONS:

Step 1: Preheat your air fryer to 180°C.

Step 2: In a large mixing bowl, combine the minced garlic, curry paste, sweet and sour sauce, and soy sauce. Mix well, then add in the wings, ensuring they are all coated evenly.

Step 3: Spray your air fryer basket and crisper tray with cooking spray, then arrange the wings in a single layer.

Step 4: Cook for about 25 minutes until cooked through. Serve hot and top with thinly sliced spring onions.

12. Simple Butter Shortbread Cookies

This extremely easy, delicately crisp, and soft melt-in-your-mouth butter shortbread recipe is super quick, delicious, and can keep for weeks when stored in an airtight container.

PREPARATION TIME: 15 MINUTES
COOKING TIME: 30 MINUTES
PER SERVING (6): KCAL: 483; FAT: 30.8G; CARBS: 48.5G; PROTEIN: 4.6G; SUGARS: 16.8G; FIBRE: 1.1G.

INGREDIENTS:

- 250g all-purpose flour
- 225g softened unsalted butter
- 100g sugar
- ½ teaspoon coarse sea salt

INSTRUCTIONS:

Step 1: Preheat your air fryer to 160°C.

Step 2: Cream the sugar, butter, and salt in the bowl of a stand mixer (using the paddle attachment) until fluffy. If you don't have a stand mixer, you can use a hand mixer or just a fork and whisk.

Step 3: Mix in the flour until just combined. Do not over-mix the dough.

Step 4: Transfer the dough to a baking pan and gently press it down. Use a fork to poke holes in the dough.

Step 5: Bake for about 30 minutes until lightly golden. Halfway through the cooking time, check on it, and if it's browning too quickly, cover the top with aluminium foil.

Step 6: Take out the large shortbread, and let it cool slightly. Cut into bars or the desired shape while still soft before allowing to cool completely.

13. Moist Chocolate Cake With Chocolate Chips

The most amazing, quick, and easy chocolate cake that is moist, rich, and has the perfect balance of fudginess and fluffiness. The icing sugar is the cherry on top!

PREPARATION TIME: 15 MINUTES
COOKING TIME: 20 MINUTES
PER SERVING (6): KCAL: 381; FAT: 15.5G; CARBS: 62.5G; PROTEIN: 3.8G; SUGARS: 40.9G; FIBRE: 3.8G.

INGRENKEDIENTS:

* 125g all-purpose flour
* ¾ teaspoon baking soda
* 50g unsweetened cocoa powder
* 4 tablespoons semisweet chocolate chips
* 200g granulated sugar
* 1 teaspoon white vinegar
* 1 teaspoon vanilla extract
* 75ml vegetable oil
* ½ teaspoon coarse sea salt
* 250ml cold water
* 2 tablespoons icing sugar, for dusting

INSTRUCTIONS:

Step 1: Preheat your air fryer to 160°C.

Step 2: Spray an 8-inch metal baking pan with non-stick cooking spray.

Step 3: Combine all the dry ingredients in a large bowl.

Step 4: Mix in the cold water and vegetable oil until you get a smooth batter. Add in the vanilla extract and white vinegar, mix well, then fold in the chocolate chips.

Step 5: Pour the batter into your baking pan and tap the bottom to ensure it spreads evenly. Top with some chocolate chips (optional).

Step 6: Bake for 20 minutes or until an inserted tester or cocktail stick at the centre comes out clean.

Step 7: Transfer the cake to a wire rack to cool off completely, then dust with icing sugar.

14. Nutty Apricot Bites

A delicious cross between cake and shortbread, these nutty apricot bites are perfectly chewy, easy to make, and oh so tasty!

PREPARATION TIME: 10 MINUTES
COOKING TIME: 30 MINUTES
PER SERVING (8): KCAL: 538; FAT: 33.2G; CARBS: 57.6G; PROTEIN: 6.7G; SUGARS: 34.5G; FIBRE: 2.6G.

INGREDIENTS:

* 160g all-purpose flour
* 140g almond paste, loosened
* 150g sugar
* 225g softened butter
* 120ml apricot jam
* 75g almonds, sliced
* 1 teaspoon almond extract
* 1 egg
* ¼ teaspoon ground cardamom
* ½ teaspoon coarse sea salt

INSTRUCTIONS:

Step 1: Preheat your air fryer to 160°C and line a metal baking pan with parchment paper. Then lightly spray with cooking spray.

Step 2: Add the almond paste to a food processor and pulse until crumbly. Add in the sugar, cardamom, and salt. Pulse until well combined, then add in the egg and softened butter, and process until smooth.

Step 3: Add the almond extract to the food processor, followed by the flour, and pulse until well combined.

Step 4: Transfer the batter to the prepared pan, spreading it evenly, then spread the apricot jam on top. Sprinkle the almond slices on top and transfer to the air fryer.

Step 5: Bake for 25–30 minutes, until the cookie base is cooked and the almonds have browned.

Step 6: Transfer to a wire rack and let it cool slightly before cutting it into desired shapes. Then let it cool completely.

15. Berry Cheesecake Bars

These bite-sized berry cheesecake bars are the ultimate dessert. The crunchiness of the Graham cracker base and the sweetness and creaminess of the cream cheese and mixed berry jam create a beautiful explosion in your taste buds.

PREPARATION TIME: 10 MINUTES
COOKING TIME: 30 MINUTES
PER SERVING (8): KCAL: 509; FAT: 31.5G; CARBS: 53.9G; PROTEIN: 7.2G; SUGARS: 48.2G; FIBRE: 0.7G.

INGRENKEDIENTS:

- 120g Graham cracker crumbs, plain or chocolate
- 225g softened cream cheese
- 6 tablespoons unsalted butter, melted
- 2 eggs
- 220g sugar
- 1 teaspoon fresh lemon juice
- 1 teaspoon lemon zest, grated
- 2 tablespoons seedless mixed berry jam

INSTRUCTIONS:

Step 1: Preheat your air fryer to 160°C.

Step 2: Line a metal 8-inch baking pan with kitchen foil, then set aside.

Step 3: Combine the crumbed Graham crackers, melted butter, and 1 tablespoon of sugar.

Step 4: Transfer this mixture to the prepared pan, gently pressing it down to make it firm.

Step 5: Combine the softened cheese, lemon juice and zest, and the remaining sugar until well combined. Then mix in the eggs.

Step 6: Spread the cream cheese mix over the crust in the baking pan. Use a fork to beat the mixed berry jam, ensuring there are no lumps, then spoon over the cream cheese mix. Use the tip of a knife to make swirls in the jam.

Step 7: Bake for 20 minutes, then let it cool and top with more jam, if desired. Chill in the fridge for 4 hours or overnight, then slice into bars ot desired shape.

16. Spongy Olive Cake

Moist with a very fresh olive oil taste, this spongy olive cake is light, spongy and has a pleasant earthy flavour. Enjoy a slice of olive cake with an afternoon cup of tea.

PREPARATION TIME: 10 MINUTES
COOKING TIME: 30 MINUTES
PER SERVING (6): KCAL: 427; FAT: 22.1G; CARBS: 54.2G; PROTEIN: 6.4G; SUGARS: 29.2G; FIBRE: 0.9G.

INGREDIENTS:

- 125g all-purpose flour
- 70g finely ground polenta
- 1 teaspoon baking powder
- 120ml olive oil
- 3 eggs
- 150g sugar
- 120ml whole milk
- ½ teaspoon sea salt
- ½ teaspoon vanilla extract
- Grated zest of 1 orange
- 2 tablespoons icing sugar, for dusting top of cake

INSTRUCTIONS:

Step 1: Preheat your air fryer to 160°C.

Step 2: Spray a baking pan with non-stick cooking spray.

Step 3: Beat the eggs and sugar in the bowl with a stand mixer or food processor until smooth. Add the oil in a slow stream and continue mixing.

Step 4: Add in the milk, grated orange zest, and vanilla extract until well mixed.

Step 5: In a separate bowl, combine the flour, polenta, salt, and baking powder.

Step 6: Add the dry ingredients to the wet ingredients and mix until just combined.

Step 7: Bake for 30 minutes until an inserted tester or cocktail stick comes out clean. Let the cake cool, then dust with icing sugar.

17. Strawberry and Cream Cheese Triangles

These strawberry and cream cheese triangles are crunchy, cheesy, delicious, and pair perfectly with red wine. Enjoy!

PREPARATION TIME: 10 MINUTES
COOKING TIME: 30 MINUTES
PER SERVING (6): KCAL: 366; FAT: 19G; CARBS: 43.8G; PROTEIN: 5G; SUGARS: 4.4G; FIBRE: 0.7G.

INGRENKEDIENTS:

- 225g puff pastry
- 5 tablespoons all-purpose flour, for rolling
- 8 tablespoons cream cheese, softened
- 170g strawberry jam
- 1 egg, beaten with a tablespoon of water
- 2 tablespoons granulated sugar

INSTRUCTIONS:

Step 1: Preheat your air fryer to 160°C.

Step 2: Carefully unfold the pastry sheet and sprinkle some flour on it. Roll it out into a rectangle of about 10 by 15 inches.

Step 3: Divide the pastry sheet into 6 equal squares, then place a heaped tablespoon of the cream cheese at the centre of each square and top with a tablespoon of strawberry jam.

Step 4: Brush the edges of the squares with the egg mix, then gently fold the pastry square in half to form a triangle. Use a fork to crimp the edges. Brush the triangles with the remaining egg mix, then sprinkle with the sugar.

Step 5: Spray your air fryer basket with non-stick cooking spray and put in the pastries. Bake for 12 minutes until golden. Serve hot or warm.

18. Crispy Tofu Bites

Crispy and flavourful, these crispy tofu bites are the perfect movie night snack. Quick and super easy to prepare, these bites are versatile and such a hit!

PREPARATION TIME: 5 MINUTES
COOKING TIME: 18 MINUTES
PER SERVING (2): KCAL: 179; FAT: 9.5G; CARBS: 14.1G; PROTEIN: 10.2G; SUGARS: 1G; FIBRE: 1.3G.

INGREDIENTS:

- 225g firm tofu, cubed
- 3 tablespoons cornflour
- 2 teaspoons rice vinegar
- 2 tablespoons soy sauce
- 2 teaspoons peanut or sesame oil

INSTRUCTIONS:

Step 1: In a large bowl combine the rice vinegar, soy sauce, and oil. Toss in the tofu cubes and marinate for 20 minutes.

Step 2: Preheat your air fryer to 190°C and press the Start/Pause button.

Step 3: Drain the excess marinade from the tofu and toss the cubes in the cornflour until evenly coated. Let the cubes rest as the cornflour absorbs the marinade on the tofu.

Step 4: Place the tofu cubes in the basket of your air fryer and lightly spray with cooking spray.

Step 5: Cook until golden for 18 minutes. You can enjoy the cubes hot, warm, or cold.

19. Classic Grilled Cheese Sandwich

There's no better comfort snack than a piping-hot, melted grilled cheese sandwich. This recipe is simple, quick, and easy. Serve with some tomato soup for the ultimate culinary experience!

PREPARATION TIME: 5 MINUTES
COOKING TIME: 18 MINUTES
PER SERVING (3): KCAL: 452; FAT: 32.4G; CARBS: 23.6G; PROTEIN: 17.4G; SUGARS: 3.3G; FIBRE: 3.8G.

INGRENKEDIENTS:

* 4 slices of your sturdy bread of choice
* 80g mature cheddar cheese, grated
* 3 tablespoons butter, softened

INSTRUCTIONS:

Step 1: Preheat your air fryer to 160°C, and press Start/ Pause.

Step 2: Apply butter on each side of the bread slices and divide the cheese evenly between 2 slices of bread. Cover with the other 2 slices to make 2 sandwiches.

Step 3: Gently place the 2 sandwiches in your air fryer basket and cook for 8–10 minutes or until golden.

Step 4: Take out the sandwiches, cut in half (diagonally or horizontally), and serve hot.

20. Crunchy Fish Nuggets

These crunchy fish nuggets are a terrific snack for adults and kids alike. They are crispy on the outside, moist and flaky on the inside. The best part about these air fryer fish nuggets is you don't need to worry about them being gr easy!

PREPARATION TIME: 15 MINUTES
COOKING TIME: 12 MINUTES
PER SERVING (4): KCAL: 369; FAT: 10.2G; CARBS: 34.6G; PROTEIN: 36.2G; SUGARS: 2.5G; FIBRE: 4.1G.

INGREDIENTS:

* 450g tilapia fillets, cut into strips
* 30g all-purpose flour
* 180g panko breadcrumbs
* 2 eggs, lightly beaten
* 1 tablespoon mixed spice seasoning
* Cooking spray
* Tartar sauce, for serving

INSTRUCTIONS:

Step 1: Combine the flour and the mixed spice seasoning in a shallow bowl. Place the beaten eggs in another shallow bowl and the panko breadcrumbs in another bowl, too.

Step 2: Coat the fish strips, one at a time, with the seasoned flour. Shake off any excess, then dip in the egg mixture and the panko breadcrumbs thereafter before placing on a platter. Repeat for the remaining fish strips.

Step 3: Preheat your air fryer to 180°C.

Step 4: Lightly spray the coated fish with cooking spray, place in the basket of your air fryer, and cook for 6 minutes. Turn the fish and cook for another 6 minutes or until golden. Serve hot with tartar sauce.

21. Crispy Tortilla Chips

Kcal: 92; Fat: 4.2g; Carbs: 12.9g; Protein: 1.9g; Sugars: 1.2g; Fibre: 2.1g.

PREPARATION TIME: 5 MINUTES
COOKING TIME: 8 MINUTES
PER SERVING (4): KCAL: 92; FAT: 4.2G; CARBS: 12.9G; PROTEIN: 1.9G; SUGARS: 1.2G; FIBRE: 2.1G.

INGREDIENTS:

- 4 corn tortillas
- 1 tablespoon olive oil
- ½ teaspoon salt
- ½ teaspoon freshly ground black pepper
- Salsa, for serving

INSTRUCTIONS:

Step 1: Stack the tortillas on top of each other on a chopping board. Cut them in half and cut the halves into quarters for a total of 32 pieces.

Step 2: Preheat your air fryer to 150°C.

Step 3: Combine the olive oil, salt, and pepper in a large bowl, then toss in the tortilla pieces until evenly coated.

Step 4: Place the pieces in your air fryer and cook for 8 minutes, tossing the tortilla pieces halfway through the cooking time.

Step 5: Serve with salsa, guacamole, or a cheese dip.

22. Air-Fried Cheese Bites

If you are a cheese lover, you are going to enjoy these crunchy and gooey air-fried cheese bites. Serve with ranch or marinara sauce. Enjoy!

PREPARATION TIME: 15 MINUTES
COOKING TIME: 15 MINUTES
PER SERVING (4): KCAL: 338; FAT: 13.6G; CARBS: 32.4G; PROTEIN: 23.1G; SUGARS: 1.1G; FIBRE: 3.7G.

INGREDIENTS:

- 8 pieces string cheese, cut into thirds
- 150g panko breadcrumbs
- 2 tablespoons all-purpose flour
- 1 teaspoon cornflour
- 2 eggs and 1 tablespoon of water, beaten
- ½ teaspoon sea salt
- ½ teaspoon freshly ground black pepper
- 1 teaspoon dried oregano
- Cooking spray

INSTRUCTIONS:

Step 1: Combine the flour, cornflour, pepper, and salt in a shallow bowl. Beat the eggs in another shallow bowl and place the breadcrumbs in another shallow bowl.

Step 2: Coat the cheese pieces in the seasoned flour, dip in the egg, and roll in the panko. Dip in the egg and panko again for a thick coating. Place the coated cheese sticks in the freezer as you wait for the air fryer to heat up.

Step 3: Preheat your air fryer to 180°C.

Step 4: Place the cheese sticks in the air fryer basket and spray with cooking spray. Cook for 10–15 minutes until crisp and golden on the outside and soft and melty on the inside. Sprinkle with dried oregano and serve.

Step 5: Serve with your favourite sauce.

23. Pickle Fries

Okay, this might sounds a little strange, but pickle fries are the real deal! Crunchy, perfectly spiced, and absolutely tasty, you will love every bite of this delicious snack.

PREPARATION TIME: 15 MINUTES
COOKING TIME: 10 MINUTES
PER SERVING (4): KCAL: 167; FAT: 3.2G; CARBS: 28.6G; PROTEIN: 6.7G; SUGARS: 1.4G; FIBRE: 3.4G.

INGRENKEDIENTS:

- 4 dill pickles, each cut into 8 sticks
- 70g all-purpose flour
- 2 eggs
- 80g panko breadcrumbs
- 1 teaspoon sweet paprika
- ½ teaspoon cayenne pepper
- Salt, to taste
- Freshly ground black pepper, to taste
- Cooking spray

INSTRUCTIONS:

Step 1: Dry the pickle sticks using paper towels.

Step 2: Add the flour to a shallow bowl and set aside. Beat the eggs in another shallow bowl, then combine the breadcrumbs, salt, and spices in another shallow bowl.

Step 3: Preheat your air fryer to 185°C.

Step 4: Dredge the pickle pieces in the flour, dip in the egg, and roll in the breadcrumbs.

Step 5: Spray the coated pickle sticks, then place in the basket of your air fryer and cook for 10 minutes, tossing halfway through the cooking time.

Step 6: Serve with your favourite sauce.

24. Fluffy Cinnamon Rolls

Make the best and tastiest fluffy cinnamon rolls from scratch with very delicious results. What's more, they only take 10 minutes in the air fryer.

PREPARATION TIME: 2 HOURS
COOKING TIME: 12 MINUTES
PER SERVING (12): KCAL: 695; FAT: 21.9G; CARBS: 111.6G; PROTEIN: 13.1G; SUGARS: 25.5G; FIBRE: 4.1G.

INGREDIENTS:

Cinnamon rolls:

- 1 cup warm milk
- ½ packet active dry yeast
- 320g all-purpose flour, divided, more for dusting
- ½ teaspoon baking powder
- 50g white sugar
- 60g unsalted butter, melted
- 1 teaspoon sea salt
- 60g unsalted butter, softened
- 110g dark brown sugar
- 3 teaspoons ground cinnamon

Frosting:

- 100g softened cream cheese
- 125g icing sugar
- 110g unsalted butter, room temperature
- ½ teaspoon vanilla extract

INSTRUCTIONS:

Step 1: Combine the milk, yeast, white sugar, and melted butter in a large glass bowl and let bloom for about 2 minutes.

Step 2: Mix in 250g of the flour until well combined. Cover with a clean towel and let sit for an hour in a warm area.

Step 3: Mix in the remaining flour, salt, and baking powder, then transfer the dough to a floured surface. Knead the dough until smooth, then roll out to about quarter-inch thickness.

Step 4: Spread the softened butter on the surface of the dough. Combine the dark brown sugar and cinnamon, then sprinkle over the dough.

Step 5: Tightly roll the dough to form a log and cut it into 1- to 2-inch slices. Place on an oiled sheet pan and cover with a clean towel. Leave it for half an hour.

Step 6: Preheat your air fryer to 160°C.

Step 7: Place the cinnamon rolls on parchment paper, then place in your air fryer and cook for 12 minutes. Meanwhile, combine all the frosting ingredients, ensuring there are no lumps, and set aside.

Step 8: Remove from the air fryer and spread with the frosting. Enjoy!

25. Yummy Air Fryer Apple Pies

These yummy air fryer apple pies are crunchy on the outside and filled with a sweet, spicy, and buttery filling, and are ready in only half an hour from start to finish.

PREPARATION TIME: 15 MINUTES
COOKING TIME: 10 MINUTES
PER SERVING (3): KCAL: 341; FAT: 11.5G; CARBS: 61.1G; PROTEIN: 2.4G; SUGARS: 51G; FIBRE: 2.2G.

INGRENKEDIENTS:

- 1 sheet pie dough
- 1 apple, peeled and cut into bite-sized pieces
- 1 tablespoon unsalted butter
- 2½ tablespoons granulated sugar
- ½ teaspoon ground allspice
- ½ teaspoon ground cinnamon
- ½ teaspoon ground nutmeg
- 1 egg and 1 teaspoon water

INSTRUCTIONS:

Step 1: Place a medium pan over medium heat and add in the apples, spices, sugar, and butter, and bring to a gentle simmer. Let it cook for 2 minutes before turning off the heat and allowing to cool completely.

Step 2: Cut 3 circles out of the dough of approximately 4–5 inches. Divide the apple mixture among the 3 circles at the centres. Use your fingers to apply water to the outer edges of the circles, then gently crimp the dough. Make a tiny split at the top of each pie.

Step 3: Preheat your air fryer to 180°C.

Step 4: Make an egg wash by beating the egg and water. Brush it onto the pies, then place the pies in the air fryer and cook for 10 minutes, turning halfway through the cooking time.

Step 5: Serve and enjoy.

26. Air Fryer Sweet Coconut Macaroons

Sweet, chewy, nutty, and sea-salt flavours... everything you'd expect from a coconut macaroon. These air fryer sweet coconut macaroons are perfectly crisp and chewy.

PREPARATION TIME: 8 MINUTES
COOKING TIME: 15 MINUTES
PER SERVING (3): KCAL: 294; FAT: 21.5G; CARBS: 23.2G; PROTEIN: 5.2G; SUGARS: 17.9G; FIBRE: 5.3G.

INGREDIENTS:

- 175g unsweetened coconut, grated, divided
- 60ml sweet condensed milk
- ¼ teaspoon vanilla extract
- ¼ teaspoon almond extract
- 1 egg white
- ¼ teaspoon sea salt

NSTRUCTIONS:

Step 1: Combine the egg white, condensed milk, vanilla extract, almond extract, and sea salt in a large bowl.

Step 2: Add in 120g and mix well, then form into balls. Coat the balls in the remaining grated coconut.

Step 3: Preheat your air fryer to 150°C.

Step 4: Cook the coconut macaroons for 15 minutes, then let them cool for about 5 minutes before serving.

27. Air Fryer Soufflé

This is the easiest, fluffiest, and most decadent chocolate soufflé you're ever going to make that is sure to be etched in your memory. With a light, gooey, and chocolaty interior and delicately crunchy in the corners and at the top, this recipe will take you straight to culinary heaven!

PREPARATION TIME: 25 MINUTES
COOKING TIME: 13 MINUTES
PER SERVING (2): KCAL: 605; FAT: 40.1G; CARBS: 52.4G; PROTEIN: 10G; SUGARS: 42.9G; FIBRE: 1.7G.

INGRENKEDIENTS:

* 90g bittersweet chocolate, cut into chunks
* 2 tablespoons all-purpose flour
* 60g unsalted butter, more for greasing
* 2 eggs, yolks and whites separated
* 3 tablespoons sugar, more for coating
* ½ teaspoon vanilla extract
* 1 teaspoon icing sugar, for dusting

INSTRUCTIONS:

Step 1: Grease 2 ramekins with butter and sprinkle some sugar over. Gently shake to spread it all round, then pour out the excess.

Step 2: Combine the chocolate and butter in a microwave-safe bowl and microwave in 15-second intervals until completely melted.

Step 3: In a medium bowl, whisk the melted chocolate, egg yolks, and vanilla extract, whisking vigorously to prevent the egg from scrambling. Whisk in the flour, ensuring there are no lumps, then let it cool.

Step 4: Meanwhile, beat the egg whites in a large glass bowl using a hand mixer until they form soft peaks. Whisk in the sugar a little at a time. Continue whisking until you get stiff peaks, then set aside.

Step 5: Preheat your air fryer to 160°C.

Step 6: Fold half the egg whites into the chocolate mix, then add the chocolate mix to the remaining egg whites and fold very gently until well combined.

Step 7: Transfer the batter into the ramekins and place the ramekins in the air fryer. Cook for 13 minutes.

Step 8: Once done, remove from the air fryer, dust with icing sugar, and serve immediately.

28. Chocolate Muffins

These chocolate muffins are moist, sweet, and chocolaty with a delicious and subtle coffee flavour. Easy to make and with an amazing combination of flavours, you are going to love every bite of these muffins.

PREPARATION TIME: 15 MINUTES
COOKING TIME: 15 MINUTES
PER SERVING (6): KCAL: 384; FAT: 21.2G; CARBS: 48.2G; PROTEIN: 6.1G; SUGARS: 26.1G; FIBRE: 3.8G.

INGREDIENTS:

* 125g all-purpose flour
* ½ teaspoon baking soda
* 60g cocoa powder
* 170g light brown sugar
* 3 tablespoons chocolate chips
* ½ teaspoon baking powder
* ½ teaspoon instant espresso powder
* ¼ teaspoon sea salt
* 1 large egg
* 180ml milk
* 1 teaspoon vanilla extract
* 1 teaspoon apple cider vinegar
* 120ml vegetable oil
* Cooking spray

INSTRUCTIONS:

Step 1: Combine the flour, baking powder, baking soda, cocoa powder, sugar, sea salt, and instant espresso powder in a large bowl until well combined.

Step 2: Combine all the wet ingredients in a separate bowl, then mix this with the dry ingredients.

Step 3: Grease the muffin cups with non-stick cooking spray, then fill the cups with batter three-quarters of the way.

Step 4: Preheat your air fryer to 150°C.

Step 5: Place the muffin cups in the air fryer and bake for 15 minutes. Remove from the air fryer and let them cool.

29. Orange Berry Muffins

These air fryer orange berry muffins are so good. Deliciously crispy on the outside and pillow soft on the inside, these muffins are the real deal.

PREPARATION TIME: 15 MINUTES
COOKING TIME: 15 MINUTES
PER SERVING (6): KCAL: 224; FAT: 10.2G; CARBS: 29G; PROTEIN: 3.1G; SUGARS: 10.5G; FIBRE: 2G.

INGRENKEDIENTS:

- 125g all-purpose flour
- ¼ teaspoon baking soda
- 50g sugar
- 1 teaspoon baking powder
- Grated zest of 1 orange
- 60ml fresh orange juice
- 60ml vegetable oil
- 200g cranberries
- 1 egg
- ¼ teaspoon sea salt

INSTRUCTIONS:

Step 1: Combine all the dry ingredients and the cranberries in a large bowl and all the wet ingredients in a separate bowl, then mix together.

Step 2: Grease the muffin cups with non-stick cooking spray, then pour in the batter three-quarters of the way.

Step 3: Preheat your air fryer to 150°C.

Step 4: Place the muffin cups in the air fryer and bake for 15 minutes. Remove from the air fryer and let them cool.

30. Choc 'N' Nut Banana Bread

This decadent banana bread is rich with chocolaty and banana sweetness and an earthy nuttiness. Moist, cakey, and deliciously soft, this is an awesome banana bread recipe.

PREPARATION TIME: 15 MINUTES
COOKING TIME: 40 MINUTES
PER SERVING (4): KCAL: 473; FAT: 24.7G; CARBS: 58.6G; PROTEIN: 9.1G; SUGARS: 32.6G; FIBRE: 3.5G.

INGREDIENTS:

- 100g all-purpose flour
- ½ teaspoon baking soda
- 2 very ripe bananas, mashed
- 75g walnuts, chopped
- 3 tablespoons chocolate chips
- 60g unsalted butter, softened
- 100g sugar
- 1 egg
- ¼ teaspoon vanilla extract
- ½ teaspoon sea salt

NSTRUCTIONS:

Step 1: Mix the butter and sugar until creamy; then whisk in the egg, vanilla extract, and mashed bananas.

Step 2: Preheat your air fryer to 150°C.

Step 3: Sift the flour, salt, and baking soda, and mix into the wet ingredients using a gentle folding motion. Next, fold in the walnuts and chocolate chips.

Step 4: Grease a mini loaf pan using non-stick cooking spray and pour in the batter. You can cook in batches or freeze the leftover batter.

Step 5: Bake the loaf for 40 minutes until an inserted tester or cocktail stick comes out clean. Remove from the air fryer and let it cool.

MEAT

Don't Forget To Get The Color Images FREE!
Simply Scan The QR Code Below!

Hello! Please scan the QR code below to access your promised bonus of all our recipes with full colored photos & beautiful designs! It is the best we could do to keep the book as cheap as possible while providing the best value!

Also, once downloaded you can take the PDF with you digitally wherever you go- meaning you can cook these recipes wherever an Air Fryer is present!

STEP BY STEP Guide-

1. *Open Your Phones (Or Any Device You Want The Book On) Back Camera. The Back Camera Is The One You use as if you are taking a picture of someone.*

2. *Simply point your Camera at the QR code and 'tap' the QR code with your finger to focus the camera.*

3. *A link / pop up will appear. Simply tap that (and make sure you have internet connection) and the FREE PDF containing all of the colored images should appear.*

4. *If You Click On The File And It Says 'The File Is Too Big To Preview' Simply click 'Download' and it will download the full book onto your phone!*

5. *Now you have access to these FOREVER. Simply 'Bookmark' The tab it opened on, or download the document and take wherever you want.*

6. *Repeat this on any device you want it on!*

Any Issues / Feedback / Troubleshooting please email:
anthonypublishing123@gmail.com *and our customer service team will help you! We want to make sure you have the BEST experience with our books!*

1. Juicy Rib-Eye Steak

This juicy rib-eye steak is so tender, juicy, and full of flavour. The best thing about this air fryer recipe is that you can cook it to your perfect level of doneness without losing its juiciness.

PREPARATION TIME: 10 MINUTES
COOKING TIME: 14 MINUTES
PER SERVING (4): KCAL: 751; FAT: 53.1G; CARBS: 6G; PROTEIN: 62.1G; SUGARS: 0.3G; FIBRE: 0.5G.

INGRENKEDIENTS:

- 450g boneless rib-eye steaks
- 1 tablespoon olive oil
- ¾ teaspoon kosher salt
- ¾ teaspoon garlic powder
- ¾ teaspoon onion powder
- ½ teaspoon dried rosemary
- ¾ teaspoon dried oregano
- ¾ teaspoon freshly ground black pepper
- ½ teaspoon cayenne pepper
- ½ teaspoon dried sage

INSTRUCTIONS:

Step 1: Preheat your air fryer to 205°C.

Step 2: Combine all the seasoning, including salt, and rub this generously on the steak, then rub with olive oil.

Step 3: Place the seasoned steak in your air fryer and cook for 14 minutes, flipping the steak halfway through.

Step 4: Let it rest for 10 minutes before serving.

2. Tender Strip Steak With Chimichurri

I pack this meatloaf with some yellow peppers, onion, and carrots to create a unison of colour, certify its healthiness, and make it better flavoured.

PREPARATION TIME: 10 MINUTES
COOKING TIME: 14 MINUTES
PER SERVING (2): KCAL: 502; FAT: 32.4G; CARBS: 8.5G; PROTEIN: 46.7G; SUGARS: 4.9G; FIBRE: 1.2G.

INGREDIENTS:

Steak:

- 450g strip steak
- 2 tablespoons olive oil
- Sea salt and black pepper, to taste

Chimichurri sauce:

- 60ml extra virgin olive oil
- 4 anchovy fillets
- 2 cloves garlic, peeled
- 1 small shallot
- 30g fresh basil
- 30g coriander
- 30g parsley
- Juice of 1 lemon
- ¼ teaspoon crushed red pepper

INSTRUCTIONS:

Step 1: Add all the chimichurri ingredients to your food processor and pulse until smooth or you achieve the desired consistency.

Step 2: Preheat your air fryer to 205°C.

Step 3: Season the steak with salt and pepper, and rub with olive oil.

Step 4: Place the seasoned steak in your air fryer and cook for 14 minutes, flipping the steak halfway through.

Step 5: Let it rest for 10 minutes before slicing and serving with the chimichurri sauce.

3. Balsamic and Mustard Flank Steak

Flank steak can be a hit or miss because it's so thin and can easily dry out. This balsamic mustard flank steak is juicy and flavourful from the marinade and cooked to perfection in the air fryer.

PREPARATION TIME: 10 MINUTES
COOKING TIME: 14 MINUTES
PER SERVING (3): KCAL: 446; FAT: 29.7G; CARBS: 0.8G; PROTEIN: 42.2G; SUGARS: 0.2G; FIBRE: 0.4G.

INGRENKEDIENTS:

- 450g flank steak
- ¼ cup olive oil
- 2 tablespoons Dijon mustard
- ¼ cup balsamic vinegar
- 4 fresh basil leaves, sliced
- Sea salt, to taste
- Freshly ground black pepper, to taste

INSTRUCTIONS:

Step 1: Mix the balsamic vinegar, olive oil, and Dijon mustard in a large bowl, and place the steak in the marinade. Cover with clingfilm and chill in the fridge for 2 hours or, better still, overnight.

Step 2: Once ready to cook, remove the steak from the fridge and let it warm up to room temperature for 30 minutes.

Step 3: Preheat your air fryer to 205°C.

Step 4: Place the marinated steak in your air fryer and cook for 14 minutes, flipping the steak halfway through.

Step 5: Let it rest for 10 minutes before serving. Slice diagonally to cut through the toughness of the muscle. Season with salt and fresh pepper, and garnish with sliced basil.

4. Classic Steak Sandwich

This classic steak sandwich is really easy to make and is deliciously juicy with a tasty cream sauce that enhances all the flavours. Perfect for a weeknight dinner; you are going to enjoy this recipe.

PREPARATION TIME: 2 HOURS
COOKING TIME: 14 MINUTES
PER SERVING (4): KCAL: 518; FAT: 34.3G; CARBS: 25.5G; PROTEIN: 25G; SUGARS: 2.8G; FIBRE: 1G.

INGREDIENTS:

- 450g boneless rib-eye steak
- 1 tablespoon olive oil
- 2 teaspoons chives, freshly chopped
- 3 tablespoons white horseradish, prepared and drained
- 1 small shallot, minced
- ½ teaspoon lemon juice
- 1 teaspoon salt
- ½ teaspoon black pepper
- 4 toasted buns, for serving
- ½ cup sour cream
- Baby rocket, for serving
- Shallots, sliced, for serving

NSTRUCTIONS:

Step 1: Preheat your air fryer to 205°C.

Step 2: Rub the steak with olive oil and season with salt and black pepper.

Step 3: Cook the steak for 14 minutes, remove from the air fryer, and let it rest for 5–10 minutes before cutting into thin slices.

Step 4: Combine the sour cream, chives, sliced shallots, and lemon juice.

Step 5: To assemble the sandwich, spread some of the sour cream sauce on the bottom buns, then top with the rocket, shallots, steak, and more cream on top. Then top with the remaining buns. Cut in half, then serve.

5. Juicy Italian Meatballs

These juicy Italian meatballs are crunchy on the outside and super moist with delicate herb flavours. Add the cheese and you've got yourself a winner. Serve with marinara sauce and a bowl of pasta.

PREPARATION TIME: 10 MINUTES
COOKING TIME: 10 MINUTES
PER SERVING (2): KCAL: 353; FAT: 19.4G; CARBS: 12.3G; PROTEIN: 31.8G; SUGARS: 2.8G; FIBRE: 1.8G.

INGRENKEDIENTS:

- 230g 85% lean minced beef
- ¼ cup panko breadcrumbs
- 1 teaspoon onion powder
- 1 teaspoon garlic powder
- 3 tablespoons mozzarella cheese plus more for serving
- 60ml milk
- 1 egg
- 1 tablespoon dried parsley
- 1½ teaspoons dried oregano
- Sea salt and black pepper to taste

INSTRUCTIONS:

Step 1: Combine all the ingredients in a large bowl and mix well, then roll out the meat mix into balls of the desired size and chill in the fridge for 10 minutes to allow the balls to firm up.

Step 2: Preheat the air fryer to 205°C.

Step 3: Take out the meatballs from the fridge and put them in the air fryer, spray them with cooking spray, and cook for 10 minutes.

Step 4: Serve hot, sprinkle with grated cheese, and serve with marinara sauce.

6. Japanese-Style Meatballs

These Japanese-style meatballs are deliciously juicy and moist with rich Asian flavours that will blow your mind. The dipping sauce brings out the intense Japanese flavour of the meatballs. Enjoy!

PREPARATION TIME: 10 MINUTES
COOKING TIME: 12 MINUTES
PER SERVING (4): KCAL: 287; FAT: 10.8G; CARBS: 10.3G; PROTEIN: 36G; SUGARS: 4.8G; FIBRE: 1.5G.

INGREDIENTS:

- 450g 85% lean minced beef
- 3 tablespoons soy sauce
- 1 tablespoon sesame oil
- 1 tablespoon miso paste
- 3 tablespoons mirin
- 1 teaspoon brown sugar
- 4 spring onions, finely chopped
- 10 fresh mint leaves, finely chopped
- 1 tablespoon water
- 1 teaspoon kosher salt
- ½ teaspoon freshly black pepper

INSTRUCTIONS:

Step 1: Combine all the ingredients apart from the water, mirin, soy sauce, brown sugar, sesame oil, in a large bowl until well mixed.

Step 2: Apply the sesame oil to your hands and divide the meat mix into 8 balls. Refrigerate the balls for 10 minutes to firm them up.

Step 3: To make the dipping sauce, combine the water, sugar, soy sauce, and mirin in a small bowl. Then cover and set aside.

Step 4: Preheat the air fryer to 205°C.

Step 5: Take out the meatballs from the fridge, put them in the air fryer, spray them with cooking spray, and cook for 12 minutes until cooked through.

Step 6: Serve hot with the prepared dipping sauce.

7. Sweetened Pork Chops

Crispy and juicy, these sweetened pork chops are ready in only 20 minutes. This is an easy and quick recipe that is absolutely delicious and one that you can enjoy with a side of veggies and mashed potatoes or sweet potato fries.

PREPARATION TIME: 10 MINUTES
COOKING TIME: 10 MINUTES
PER SERVING (4): KCAL: 343; FAT: 11.4G; CARBS: 13.3G; PROTEIN: 45.7G; SUGARS: 9.8G; FIBRE: 1.5G.

INGRENKEDIENTS:

* 600g pork chops
* 1 teaspoon ground mustard
* 2 teaspoons sweet paprika
* 1 teaspoon garlic powder
* 1 teaspoon onion powder
* 2 teaspoons olive oil
* 2 tablespoons dark brown sugar
* 1 teaspoon freshly ground black pepper
* Kosher salt, to taste

INSTRUCTIONS:

Step 1: Preheat the air fryer to 205°C.

Step 2: Rub the chops with olive oil. Combine the seasoning in a small bowl and liberally rub the mix on the oiled pork chops.

Step 3: Cook the chops for 10 minutes, flipping halfway through the cooking time.

Step 4: Remove the cooked pork chops and let them rest for 5 minutes before serving.

8. Delicious Boneless Pork Chops

Delicious, crispy, and juicy, these pork chops are fun and easy to make and you can use your own flavour combo to make them more personalised.

PREPARATION TIME: 15 MINUTES
COOKING TIME: 14 MINUTES
PER SERVING (3): KCAL: 393; FAT: 7.9G; CARBS: 40.4G; PROTEIN: 38.8G; SUGARS: 1.6G; FIBRE: 3.9G.

INGREDIENTS:

* 340g boneless pork chops
* 2 eggs, lightly beaten
* 100g panko breadcrumbs
* 60g all-purpose flour
* ¼ teaspoon white pepper
* 1 teaspoon onion powder
* 1 teaspoon garlic powder
* 1 teaspoon kosher salt

INSTRUCTIONS:

Step 1: Place the boneless chops in a zip-lock bag and pound using a rolling pin until you get half an inch thickness.

Step 2: Combine the breadcrumbs with all the seasoning and salt in a small bowl. Dredge the pounded chops in the flour, followed by dipping in the beaten eggs, then roll in the seasoned breadcrumb mixture.

Step 3: Preheat the air fryer to 185°C.

Step 4: Lightly spray the coated pork chops with cooking spray and cook for 14 minutes, flipping halfway through the cooking time.

Step 5: Remove the cooked chops and let them rest for 5 minutes before serving.

9. Lamb With Orange and Olives

This lamb with orange and olives is one of those meals you cook when you have a special event, like a date or when you have guests coming over. Juicy and tender with a burst of delicious flavours, this lamb dish is absolutely amazing.

PREPARATION TIME: 1 HOUR
COOKING TIME: 20 MINUTES
PER SERVING (3): KCAL: 305; FAT: 15G; CARBS: 7.9G; PROTEIN: 30.8G; SUGARS: 2.9G; FIBRE: 1.8G.

INGRENKEDIENTS:

- 4 100g boneless lamb pieces
- 200g green olives, pitted
- 1 tablespoon olive oil
- Kosher salt and ground black pepper

For the marinade:

- 80ml white wine
- 120ml orange juice
- 1 tablespoon olive oil
- ¾ teaspoon fennel seed, coarsely ground
- ¾ teaspoon crushed red pepper flakes
- ¾ teaspoon freshly ground black pepper
- ½ teaspoon sea salt
- 2 teaspoons garlic, minced
- 2 teaspoons fresh marjoram, chopped

INSTRUCTIONS:

Step 1: Preheat your air fryer to 190°C.

Step 2: Combine all the marinade ingredients in a large bowl and reserve half of it. Add the lamb to the bowl, cover, and marinate for an hour in the fridge.

Step 3: Take out the lamb from the marinade and pat dry with paper towels. Spray the air fryer basket with cooking spray and cook for 15 minutes, turning halfway through the cooking time.

Step 4: Meanwhile, add the reserved marinade and the pitted olives to a small saucepan over medium to high heat and bring to a boil. Then lower the heat to medium and let simmer for 5 minutes.

Step 5: Serve the cooked lamb and drizzle with the olive sauce. Enjoy!

10. Mint-Infused Lamb Chops

These mint-infused lamb chops are elegant enough for a night of entertaining and simple enough for a busy weeknight. They are moist, super tender, and deeply flavourful with a fresh minty taste.

PREPARATION TIME: 1 HOUR
COOKING TIME: 20 MINUTES
PER SERVING (3): KCAL: 293; FAT: 20.7G; CARBS: 2.3G; PROTEIN: 23.8G; SUGARS: 0.3G; FIBRE: 1G.

INGREDIENTS:

- 4 bone-in lamb rib chops

For the marinade:

- 40g fresh mint, finely chopped
- 20g parsley, finely chopped
- 50ml lemon juice
- 3 tablespoons olive oil
- 3 garlic cloves, finely chopped
- ½ teaspoon kosher salt
- ½ teaspoon freshly ground black pepper

INSTRUCTIONS:

Step 1: Preheat your air fryer to 205°C.

Step 2: Combine all the marinade ingredients in a large bowl and reserve half of the marinade in a smaller bowl. Mix in the lamb chops in the large bowl, cover, and marinate in the fridge for 1 hour.

Step 3: Remove the chops from the fridge and drain off the excess marinade.

Step 4: Cook the chops for 12 minutes, turning halfway through the cooking time.

Step 5: Remove the chops from the air fryer and let them rest for 5 minutes. Serve with the reserved marinade.

11. Pork and Veggie Balls

These pork and veggie balls are juicy, insanely flavourful, and versatile. You can serve them as a side dish, a snack, or party food. Enjoy!

PREPARATION TIME: 15 MINUTES
COOKING TIME: 12 MINUTES
PER SERVING (4): KCAL: 253; FAT: 6.6G; CARBS: 14.5G; PROTEIN: 32.2G; SUGARS: 1.3G; FIBRE: 0.6G.

INGREDIENTS:

- 450g ground pork
- 3 tablespoons panko breadcrumbs
- 110g water chestnuts, finely minced
- 1 egg and 1 tablespoon water lightly beaten
- 1 large spring onion, minced
- 1 garlic clove, minced
- 1 inch ginger, minced
- 1 tablespoon dark soy sauce
- Freshly ground black pepper, to taste
- Sea salt to taste
- 1 teaspoon sesame oil

INSTRUCTIONS:

Step 1: Preheat your air fryer to 205°C.

Step 2: Combine all the ingredients until well mixed and form into medium-sized balls.

Step 3: Spray the air fryer basket with non-stick cooking spray. Arrange the balls in a single layer and cook for 12 minutes.

Step 4: Serve hot over a bed of rice or pasta.

12. Spicy Spanish Pork Burgers

This spicy Spanish pork burgers recipe is perfect for those days when you are craving a restaurant-style burger. It's healthy, juicy, deeply flavourful, and ready in 36 minutes from start to finish.

PREPARATION TIME: 20 MINUTES
COOKING TIME: 16 MINUTES
PER SERVING (4): KCAL: 510; FAT: 20.2G; CARBS: 42.2G; PROTEIN: 38G; SUGARS: 3.2G; FIBRE: 3.1G.

INGREDIENTS:

For the burger:

- 450g ground pork
- 4 burger buns, optional
- 1 teaspoon sea salt
- 60g softened butter

For the citrus dressing:

- 1 tablespoon coriander, finely chopped
- 120ml whole milk yoghurt
- Zest of 1 nectarine
- ½ teaspoon sea salt

For the spice rub:

- 1 tablespoon sweet paprika
- 2 teaspoons dried coriander
- ½ teaspoon cayenne pepper
- 1 teaspoon cumin
- 1 teaspoon freshly ground black pepper
- 1 teaspoon sea salt

INSTRUCTIONS:

Step 1: Combine all the spice rub ingredients in a small bowl and mix well.

Step 2: Combine all the burger ingredients and form into 4 equal-sized burger patties. Liberally coat with the spice rub.

Step 3: Preheat the air fryer to 190°C.

Step 4: Cook the burgers for 16 minutes, flipping them halfway through the cooking time.

Step 5: Slice the buns horizontally, toast them, and spread butter on them. Meanwhile, combine all the dressing ingredients.

Step 6: Assemble the burgers and drizzle with the dressing before adding the bun tops. You can also serve with a slice of Manchego cheese for a greater infusion of flavour.

13. Roasted Pepper Burgers

These roasted pepper burgers have an amazing earthy flavour, are super moist, and are delicious; perfect for a weekend night with some chips and a side of fresh salad.

PREPARATION TIME: 20 MINUTES
COOKING TIME: 36 MINUTES
PER SERVING (4): KCAL: 462; FAT: 21.2G; CARBS: 27.2G; PROTEIN: 39.6G; SUGARS: 6G; FIBRE: 1.9G.

INGRENKEDIENTS:

* 2 large poblano peppers
* 4 hamburger buns
* 60g softened butter

For the burger:

* 450g ground beef
* 1 teaspoon garlic powder
* 1 teaspoon kosher salt

For the salsa:

* 150g salsa
* 1 tablespoon ketchup

INSTRUCTIONS:

Step 1: Start by cooking the peppers, when whole, in the air fryer at 205°C for 15 minutes, turning halfway through the cooking time. The remove from the air fryer and cover for 20 minutes before peeling off the skin, removing the seeds, and chopping finely.

Step 2: Combine the burger ingredients, mix in the chopped peppers, then shape into 4 patties.

Step 3: Cook the burgers in the air fryer at 205°C for 16 minutes, turning them 8 minutes into the cooking time.

Step 4: Slice the buns horizontally, toast them, and spread butter on them. Assemble the burgers and top with the salsa and bun tops. Enjoy!

14. Crab-Stuffed Sirloin Steak

This crab-stuffed sirloin steak is super delicious and classy. Ready in 50 minutes from start to finish, this is the perfect steak recipe for one of those special nights. Serve with some steamed veggies and either mashed potatoes, pasta, noodles, or rice.

PREPARATION TIME: 25 MINUTES
COOKING TIME: 25 MINUTES
PER SERVING (4): KCAL: 739; FAT: 44.6G; CARBS: 8.5G; PROTEIN: 81.7G; SUGARS: 2.1G; FIBRE: 1.5G.

INGREDIENTS:

* 4 225g boneless sirloin steaks
* 225g lump crabmeat
* 40g baby spinach
* 1 red pepper, finely diced
* 40g spring onions, diced
* 1 garlic clove, minced
* 1 tablespoon olive oil
* 1 tablespoon freshly ground black pepper
* 1 tablespoon kosher salt

For the seasoned crab filling:

* 1 teaspoon seafood seasoning
* ¼ teaspoon freshly ground black pepper
* ¼ teaspoon kosher salt
* 1 egg, lightly beaten
* 60g softened cream cheese
* 2 tablespoons olive oil
* 2 tablespoons breadcrumbs

NSTRUCTIONS:

Step 1: Start by slicing pockets on the side of the steaks and generously season each steak with kosher salt and freshly ground black pepper.

Step 2: In a non-stick pan over medium heat, add the olive oil. For 1–2 minutes, sauté the garlic, pepper, spring onions, and baby spinach until just wilted, then remove from the heat.

Step 3: Mix the crab filling ingredients into the now-cooled pan until very well combined.

Step 4: Preheat your air fryer to 190°C.

Step 5: Stuff each steak with the filling and brush the steaks with olive oil. Cook in the preheated air fryer for 25 minutes, gently flipping them halfway through the cooking time.

Step 6: Let the cooked steaks rest for 5 minutes before serving.

15. Coffee Rub Pork Tenderloins

Juicy, moist, delicately sweet, and with a beautiful coffee aroma, these coffee rub pork tenderloins are the real deal!

PREPARATION TIME: 10 MINUTES
COOKING TIME: 20 MINUTES
PER SERVING (2): KCAL: 556; FAT: 12.5G; CARBS: 18.1G; PROTEIN: 89.1G; SUGARS: 11.1G; FIBRE: 1.8G.

INGRENKEDIENTS:

*   2 180g tenderloins

For the coffee and spice rub:

*   2 tablespoons ground dark coffee
*   1 tablespoon onion powder
*   1 tablespoon garlic powder
*   2 tablespoons brown sugar
*   1 tablespoon dried coriander
*   1 tablespoon freshly ground black pepper
*   1 tablespoon cumin
*   1 tablespoon sea salt

INSTRUCTIONS:

Step 1: Preheat your air fryer to 190°C.

Step 2: Mix all the coffee and spice rub ingredients in a medium bowl until very well combined.

Step 3: Generously rub the pork with the spice mix, place in your preheated air fryer's basket, and cook for 20 minutes, turning them halfway through.

Step 4: Remove the cooked pork from the air fryer and let them rest for 5 minutes before serving.

16. Cuban-Style Pork Chops

These Cuban-style pork chops go really well with rice and yellow beans. The juiciness and subtle sweetness of the chops is just amazing!.

PREPARATION TIME: 1 HOUR
COOKING TIME: 20 MINUTES
PER SERVING (6): KCAL: 436; FAT: 25.3G; CARBS: 11.9G; PROTEIN: 39.9G; SUGARS: 8.8G; FIBRE: 0.5G.

INGREDIENTS:

*   600g boneless pork chops
*   2 tablespoons softened butter
*   2 tablespoons flour

For the marinade:

*   250ml mango nectar
*   60ml extra virgin olive oil
*   ½ teaspoon cumin
*   2 tablespoons coriander, chopped and divided
*   4 teaspoons garlic, minced
*   1 teaspoon freshly ground black pepper
*   2 tablespoons fresh lime juice
*   Zest of 1 lime

NSTRUCTIONS:

Step 1: Combine all the marinade ingredients in a large bowl, leaving 2 teaspoons of coriander for garnish. Marinate the pork chops in your fridge for one hour, flipping after 30 minutes.

Step 2: If your air fryer has 2 racks, fit them in, if not, you'll need to cook in 2 batches. Preheat your air fryer to 190°C.

Step 3: Drain off the excess marinade from the chops, reserving for later. Put the chops in the air fryer and cook for 18 minutes. Rotate the racks after 9 minutes of cooking time.

Step 4: Add the marinade to a pan over medium heat and bring to a boil. Whisk the flour into the pan and cook for 2 minutes until the sauce becomes thick.

Step 5: Serve the pork chops, drizzle the sauce on top, and garnish with the reserved coriander.

17. Filet Mignon Wrapped in Bacon

This tender and extra juicy steak wrapped in crispy bacon is a steak lover's paradise. The recipe is really simple and quick, and the sauce ties all the flavours together in the most beautiful way.

PREPARATION TIME: 15 MINUTES
COOKING TIME: 25 MINUTES
PER SERVING (3): KCAL: 604; FAT: 42.7G; CARBS: 6.6G; PROTEIN: 44.2G; SUGARS: 2.1G; FIBRE: 1.6G.

INGRENKEDIENTS:

- 3 170g filet mignons
- 6 slices bacon
- 1 large yellow onion, trimmed, peeled, sliced, and separated into rings
- 1 tablespoon freshly ground black pepper
- 1 tablespoon kosher salt

For the sauce:

- 4 tablespoons fresh thyme, finely chopped
- 60g softened cream cheese
- Diced onion

INSTRUCTIONS:

Step 1: Generously season the steaks with freshly ground black pepper and salt.

Step 2: Gently place each steak into an onion ring and wrap with 2 slices of bacon, securing it with a cocktail stick.

Step 3: Preheat the air fryer to 205°C.

Step 4: Cook for 20 minutes, flipping the fillets halfway through the cooking time.

Step 5: Let the steaks rest for 5 minutes. Meanwhile, dice the remaining onion rings, caramelise in some oil in a pan over medium heat, then remove from the heat. Mix in the fresh thyme and softened cream cheese, and serve with the wrapped steak.

18. Steak in Mushroom and Red Wine Sauce

The rich flavour of the strip steak pairs so beautifully with the juicy and savoury mushrooms. Ready in only 35 minutes, this elegant recipe is a must-cook.

PREPARATION TIME: 15 MINUTES
COOKING TIME: 35 MINUTES
PER SERVING (2): KCAL: 625; FAT: 29.5G; CARBS: 15.9G; PROTEIN: 45G; SUGARS: 5.4G; FIBRE: 3.4G.

INGREDIENTS:

- 2 200g strip steaks
- 150g cremini mushrooms, sliced
- 1 sprig tarragon
- 120ml beef broth
- 350ml red wine
- 2 tablespoons butter
- 2 tablespoons olive oil
- 2 tablespoons ground fennel
- ½ tablespoons freshly ground black pepper
- ½ tablespoons sea salt

NSTRUCTIONS:

Step 1: Generously season the steaks with salt and freshly ground pepper, then rub with the fennel.

Step 2: Preheat the air fryer to 205°C.

Step 3: Meanwhile, add the butter to a pan over medium-high heat and sauté the mushrooms until soft. Stir in the broth, red wine, and the sprig of tarragon. Bring to a boil, then simmer for 15–20 minutes or until the sauce reduces by about a third.

Step 4: Gently rub the steaks with olive oil, place them in the rack of your air fryer, and cook for 15 minutes, flipping halfway through the cooking time.

Step 5: Take out the steaks and let them rest for 5 minutes.

Step 6: Serve the steaks and spoon over the sauce.

19. Restaurant-Style Rib-Eye Steak

This air fryer restaurant-style rib-eye steak is as good as it gets. It's juicy, tender, and buttery with beautiful flavours from the delicious seasoned butter.

PREPARATION TIME: 25 MINUTES
COOKING TIME: 15 MINUTES
PER SERVING (2): KCAL: 539; FAT: 44.6G; CARBS: 4.7G; PROTEIN: 0.6G; SUGARS: 0.1G; FIBRE: 0.5G.

INGRENKEDIENTS:

- 2 450g rib-eye steaks
- 2 tablespoons meat rub seasoning

Seasoned butter:

- 110g softened butter
- 1 teaspoon Dijon mustard
- 1 tablespoon fresh lemon juice
- 1 small shallot, minced
- 1 teaspoon garlic, minced
- 1 tablespoon tarragon, chopped
- 1 tablespoon fresh parsley, finely chopped
- 1 tablespoon fresh rosemary, chopped
- ¼ teaspoon freshly ground black pepper
- ¼ teaspoon sea salt

INSTRUCTIONS:

Step 1: Combine all the seasoned butter ingredients and mix until well combined. Transfer to a sheet of clingfilm and gently shape the butter into a log. Wrap with the clingfilm and chill in the fridge for it to firm up.

Step 2: Preheat your air fryer to 205°C.

Step 3: Rub the steaks with the meat rub, then place on a rack in your air fryer. Cook for 15 minutes, flipping halfway through the cooking time.

Step 4: To serve, take out the steak and place on serving plates. Cut a quarter-inch slice of butter and place on top of each steak. Let them rest for 5 minutes. Enjoy!

20. Spicy Rib-Eye Steak

This juicy and spicy rib-eye steak pairs perfectly with fresh salad and avocado. The creaminess of the avocado cuts the spice of the steak so beautifully and the fresh salad is a great palate cleanser.

PREPARATION TIME: 10 MINUTES
COOKING TIME: 15 MINUTES
PER SERVING (3): KCAL: 660; FAT: 44.5G; CARBS: 5.6G; PROTEIN: 0.6G; SUGARS: 3.2G; FIBRE: 1.6G.

INGREDIENTS:

- 3 450g rib-eye steaks
- 2 tablespoons kosher salt

Spice rub:

- 2 tablespoons spicy BBQ powder
- ½ tablespoon cumin
- 1 tablespoon sweet paprika
- ½ tablespoon cinnamon
- 1 tablespoon dark brown sugar

INSTRUCTIONS:

Step 1: Rub the steaks with a generous amount of kosher salt and set aside.

Step 2: Combine all the spice rub ingredients and rub 2 tablespoons of it on the steaks.

Step 3: Preheat the air fryer to 190°C.

Step 4: Place the steaks on the racks of your air fryer and spray with non-stick cooking spray. Cook for 15 minutes, flipping halfway through the cooking time.

Step 5: Take out the steaks from the air fryer and let them rest for 5 minutes before serving.

21. Dark Spicy Hanger Steak

This dark spicy steak is super juicy and tender. The best way to enjoy this steak is to let it cool completely, then slice it and use it to make a salad or a sandwich.

PREPARATION TIME: 10 MINUTES
COOKING TIME: 15 MINUTES
PER SERVING (2): KCAL: 490; FAT: 27.9G; CARBS: 39.8G; PROTEIN: 21.2G; SUGARS: 6.4G; FIBRE: 7.5G.

INGRENKEDIENTS:

- 2 250g hanger steaks
- 1 tablespoon kosher salt

Dark spice rub:

- 1 tablespoon sweet paprika
- ½ teaspoon dark chilli powder
- 1 teaspoon onion powder
- 1 tablespoon garlic powder
- ½ teaspoon cayenne pepper
- 1 teaspoon freshly ground black pepper
- 1 tablespoon dried thyme

INSTRUCTIONS:

Step 1: Rub the steaks with a generous amount of kosher salt and set aside.

Step 2: Combine the spice rub ingredients and liberally apply on the steaks.

Step 3: Preheat the air fryer to 190°C.

Step 4: Place the steaks on the racks of your air fryer and spray with non-stick cooking spray. Cook for 15 minutes, flipping halfway through the cooking time.

Step 5: Take out the steaks from the air fryer, and let them cool before slicing thinly for a sandwich or salad.

22. Creamy Black Pepper Steak

Super spicy and creamy, this black pepper steak is super juicy, hot, and flavourful. If you find black peppercorn too strong for your liking, you can season the steak with a little bit of the ground form or just salt.

PREPARATION TIME: 15 MINUTES
COOKING TIME: 20 MINUTES
PER SERVING (2): KCAL: 608; FAT: 44.4G; CARBS: 18.9G; PROTEIN: 19.8G; SUGARS: 1.2G; FIBRE: 6.6G.

INGREDIENTS:

- 2 400g strip steaks
- 50g black peppercorn, crushed

For the sauce:

- 60ml heavy cream
- 60ml brandy
- 2 tablespoons olive oil
- 10ml beef broth
- 3 tablespoons butter
- 1 small shallot, finely chopped
- 1 teaspoon kosher salt

NSTRUCTIONS:

Step 1: Season the steaks with salt and set aside. Layer the peppercorns on a plate and place the steaks on top, ensuring they are evenly coated, then drizzle with olive oil.

Step 2: Preheat the air fryer to 205°C.

Step 3: Cook the steaks for 12 minutes, flipping halfway through the cooking time.

Step 4: Meanwhile, add the butter to a pan over medium-high heat and sauté the shallots. Mix in the broth, brandy, and heavy cream. Once it comes to a boil, lower the heat and let the sauce thicken for about 5–8 minutes.

Step 5: Take out the steaks from the air fryer and let them rest for 5 minutes before serving with the sauce.

23. Pork Loin With Veggies

This pork loin and veggies recipe is simple and very tasty. The pork fat cooks the veggies to perfection while the pork itself is crispy on the outside and very juicy on the inside.

PREPARATION TIME: 10 MINUTES
COOKING TIME: 40 MINUTES
PER SERVING (4): KCAL: 400; FAT: 18.3G; CARBS: 13.9G; PROTEIN: 44.8G; SUGARS: 3.6G; FIBRE: 3.3G.

INGRENKEDIENTS:

- 600g pork loin roast, uncooked
- 1 tablespoon olive oil
- 3 teaspoons kosher salt
- 3 teaspoons freshly ground black pepper
- 1 medium courgette, cut into chunks and layers separated
- 1 red onion, peeled and cut into chunks
- 1 yellow squash, cut into chunks
- 2 teaspoons fresh oregano, chopped

INSTRUCTIONS:

Step 1: In a large bowl, combine the courgette, onion, squash, 1 teaspoon each of salt and pepper, the olive oil, and oregano.

Step 2: Preheat the air fryer to 160°C.

Step 3: Place the veggies on the crisper of your air fryer, place the pork fat-side down on the veggies, and cook for 40 minutes. Halfway through cooking time, stir the veggies and flip the pork, then continue cooking.

Step 4: Take out the meat and let them rest for 10 minutes before serving with the veggies.

24. Air Fryer Beef and Broccoli

So flavourful, tender, and juicy, this air fryer beef and broccoli is quick and easy to prepare, making it perfect for a weeknight. It pairs really well with white rice or noodles.

PREPARATION TIME: 1 HOUR
COOKING TIME: 15 MINUTES
PER SERVING (4): KCAL: 349; FAT: 10.8G; CARBS: 19.6G; PROTEIN: 41.9G; SUGARS: 13.6G; FIBRE: 1.9G.

INGREDIENTS:

- 450g sirloin steak, sliced thinly
- 1 broccoli head, cut into florets
- 340g teriyaki sauce
- 60ml soy sauce
- 1 tablespoon garlic powder
- 1 tablespoon canola oil
- 1 teaspoon crushed red pepper
- 1 teaspoon freshly ground black pepper
- 1 teaspoon sea salt

INSTRUCTIONS:

Step 1: Combine 180ml of the teriyaki sauce, soy sauce, garlic powder, crushed red pepper, and the meat slices in a zip-lock bag. Shake well to combine and marinate in the fridge for at least an hour or up to overnight.

Step 2: Meanwhile, toss the broccoli florets with salt, freshly ground pepper, and canola oil, and preheat the air fryer to 190°C.

Step 3: Place a crisper in the air fryer and place the broccoli in the air fryer. Cook for 15 minutes. After 5 minutes into the cooking time, take the crisper out and push the broccoli to one side. Place the meat slices on the other side and continue cooking.

Step 4: Serve the beef and broccoli with the remaining teriyaki sauce over a bed of rice or noodles.

25. Beef Empanadas

These air fryer empanadas are such a life saver. They are quick and easy to whip up and are super delicious too. You can serve them at parties as a snack and as a side to your favourite dinner.

PREPARATION TIME: 1 HOUR
COOKING TIME: 15 MINUTES
PER SERVING (2): KCAL: 458; FAT: 31.8G; CARBS: 31.5G; PROTEIN: 10.8G; SUGARS: 1.1G; FIBRE: 3.2G.

INGRENKEDIENTS:

- 200g 85% lean minced beef
- 375g shortcrust pastry, ready rolled
- 1 egg yolk
- 1 tablespoon olive oil
- 4 spring onions, finely chopped
- 1 tablespoon sweet paprika
- Sea salt, to taste
- Freshly ground black pepper, to taste

INSTRUCTIONS:

Step 1: Cook the mince in olive oil in a pan over medium heat. Season the meat with salt, sweet paprika, and pepper. Cook for 8 minutes until evenly browned, then let it cool and mix in the spring onions.

Step 2: Unroll the shortcrust pastry and cut out 8 medium-sized circles. Spoon the meat at the centre of the circles and fold in half. Mix the yolk with a tablespoon of water and brush it around the edges of the circles to help seal the empanadas. Use a fork to crimp the edges, then brush the tops with egg wash.

Step 3: Preheat the air fryer to 180°C, and once hot, place the empanadas in the air fryer. Lightly spray with non-stick cooking spray and cook for 10 minutes. Serve hot. Enjoy!

26. Simple and Healthy Beef Burger

These simple and healthy beef burgers are tasty, filling, and very easy to put together. If you're a cheese lover, you can add a slice of your favourite cheese on your burger too. Enjoy!

PREPARATION TIME: 10 MINUTES
COOKING TIME: 11 MINUTES
PER SERVING (6): KCAL: 428; FAT: 12.4G; CARBS: 60.9G; PROTEIN: 16.7G; SUGARS: 2.9G; FIBRE: 4.1G.

INGREDIENTS:

- 900g 85% lean minced beef
- 2 tablespoons olive oil
- 1 clove of garlic, minced
- 3 teaspoons soy sauce
- 6 burger buns
- 6 large lettuce leaves
- 2 tomatoes, sliced
- Salt and pepper, to taste

NSTRUCTIONS:

Step 1: In a large bowl, mix the minced beef, minced garlic, salt, pepper, olive oil, and soy sauce until well combined. Then form 6 equal-sized patties.

Step 2: Preheat your air fryer to 180°C.

Step 3: Once hot, cook the patties for 8 minutes, flipping halfway through or until cooked to your desired doneness. Take the burgers out and keep them warm.

Step 4: Place the buns in the air fryer (you may have to squash them down a little for them to fit) and toast for 3 minutes before taking them out.

Step 5: Slice the burger buns and assemble the burgers, starting with the lettuce and followed by the burger, tomato slices, and the bun tops. Serve immediately.

27. Herbed Beef Koftas

Moist and insanely flavourful, these herbed beef koftas are so easy to make, ready in a total of 18 minutes, and you can batch cook them for your weeknight beef dinners.

PREPARATION TIME: 10 MINUTES
COOKING TIME: 8 MINUTES
PER SERVING (3): KCAL: 398; FAT: 16.3G; CARBS: 3.8G; PROTEIN: 56.1G; SUGARS: 1.6G; FIBRE: 1.9G.

INGRENKEDIENTS:

*   550g minced beef
*   1 tablespoon olive oil
*   1 red onion, finely chopped
*   2 tablespoons coriander, finely chopped
*   1 teaspoon cumin
*   1 tablespoon Arabic spice mix
*   Salt and pepper, to taste

INSTRUCTIONS:

Step 1: Sauté the shallots in olive oil in a pan over medium heat, then remove from the heat and combine all the ingredients. Form 15 oval-shaped patties, then set aside.

Step 2: Preheat the air fryer to 180°C.

Step 3: Place the patties in your air fryer basket (you may have to work in batches), and cook for 8 minutes, flipping them halfway through the cooking time.

Step 4: Serve hot with a side of veggies.

28. Lemon-Infused Lamb Chops

This lemon-infused lamb chops recipe is fancy and requires very little effort. The richness of the lamb meat with the bright citrus flavour of lemon and the freshness of the garlic make this an absolutely amazing dish.

PREPARATION TIME: 10 MINUTES
COOKING TIME: 10 MINUTES
PER SERVING (4): KCAL: 491; FAT: 21.5G; CARBS: 1G; PROTEIN: 69.1G; SUGARS: 0G; FIBRE: 0.1G.

INGREDIENTS:

*   12 lamb chops
*   1 tablespoon olive oil
*   Juice and zest of 1 lemon
*   4 cloves of garlic, minced
*   Salt and pepper, to taste

NSTRUCTIONS:

Step 1: Combine the lemon zest, minced garlic, and olive oil. Rub all over the lamb chops and season well with salt and pepper, then cover and marinate for at least 2 hours.

Step 2: Preheat the air fryer to 180°C.

Step 3: Once hot, place the lamb chops in your air fryer's basket and cook for 10 minutes (you may have to cook in batches), flipping halfway through the cooking time.

Step 4: Serve hot.

AIR FRYER COOKING CHART

Food	Temperature °C	Minutes
Veggies		
Asparagus	205	7–9
Beetroots, diced	160	26–30
Bell peppers, sliced	180	8–10
Broccoli florets	205	6–8
Brussels sprouts	190	14–16
Butternut squash, halved	180	45–55
Carrots, cut into large chunks	190	25
Cauliflower florets	190	12–14
Courgettes, diced	205	17–20
Kale	190	3–5
Mushrooms, sliced	205	8–10
Meats and seafood		
Bacon slices	180	6–9
Boneless chicken breasts	180	20
Bone-in chicken thighs	190	18–20
Chicken drumsticks	205	18–22
Chicken nuggets	205	7–9
Eggs, hard-boiled	135	13–15
Eggs, soft-boiled	135	9–11
Hot dogs	200	8–10
Meatballs	205	11–13
Pork belly, diced	205	17–20
Pork chops, boneless	205	12–15
Pork chops, bone in	190	12–15
Pork loins, 500g	205	20–23
Prawns	205	4–5
Salmon fillets, 170g	205	8–11
Sausages, 170g	190	18–20
Steak, flank	205	6–8
Steak, rib-eye	205	13–18
Steak, sirloin	205	10–13
White fish	190	6–9
Frozen foods		
Cheese sticks	205	7–8
Chicken nuggets	205	10–12
Chips (potatoes)	205	16–18
Fish fingers	205	7–8
Meatballs	200	10–12
Mini pizzas/pies	180	8–11
Pizza rolls	190	7–9

Printed in Great Britain
by Amazon

20904057R00054